D0585737

THE MALT WHISKY CELLAR BOOK

THE MALT WHISKY CELLAR BOOK

NEIL WILSON

FOREWORD BY WALLACE MILROY

NEIL WILSON PUBLISHING • GLASGOW • SCOTLAND

First published by
Neil Wilson Publishing Ltd
303a The Pentagon Centre
36 Washington Street
GLASGOW
G3 8AZ
Tel: 0141-221-1117
Fax: 0141-221-5363
E-mail: nwp@cqm.co.uk
http://www.nwp.co.uk/

A catalogue record for this book is available from the British Library.

ISBN 1-897784-56-2

Typeset in Erhardt and designed by Mark Blackadder

Payhembury Marbled Papers, Upper Moultavie Cottages, BOATH
Alness, Ross-shire, IV17 0XJ. Tel/fax: 01349-883858

Printed by Cromwell Press, Trowbridge

CONTENTS

FOREWORD

This is a golden opportunity for whisky enthusiasts, be they beginners or self-confessed aficionados, not only to jot down impressions of whiskies nosed and tasted, but also to create a record to which they can refer in years to come.

No two malts are the same and like Neil I am constantly learning from new distillations and expressions. Part and parcel of the pleasure of sampling a malt, be it from a new distillery such as Lochranza, or a well-established one like Glenlivet, is the way in which the whiskies convey the nature of Scotland to the palate; an encapsulation of the place in which they are made and the age-old craft of distillation. When these factors are allied to modern techniques and processes, the result is magical.

Today we have around 80 working distilleries throughout Scotland although the number of plants capable of distilling malt whisky currently exceeds 110. Even with these figures to hand, we are now exposed to more bottlings of malt whisky than at any other time and *The Malt Whisky Cellar Book* will prove to be an invaluable resource for anyone who is inclined to sample the product of each and every malt whisky distillery. I have no doubt that in time the book will also bring back warm memories of a distant dram, perhaps drunk in a particular place or in the company of special friends.

When Alfred Barnard visited the distilleries of the United Kingdom in the 1880s he made one mistake...he did not take any tasting notes and so our direct knowledge of those late-Victorian drams is less than it could have been. Don't make the same mistake as he did. If you come across a rare bottle of malt, ensure that you have the cellar book to hand to record those vital impressions for posterity. I commend Neil's book to you and hope that through it you will gain as much pleasure from the *cratur* as I have.

Wallace Milroy, London, February 1999

PART ONE

I

HOW TO USE THE CELLAR BOOK

My interest in malt whisky has been largely due to circumstances outside my control. In the early 1980s I travelled to Islay on the spur of the moment having missed the ferry for an impromptu visit to Barra. After a few days discovering the island, I found myself asking the question: 'Why are there so many distilleries here?' and in order to answer it I spent all my free time during the next four years researching the establishment, development and current status of the industry in Islay and the Hebrides. The story might have ended there had I not developed a taste for the fantastic variety of island malts at the same time. Since that first journey of discovery, I have been introduced to some extraordinary whiskies through my activities on whisky-related matters.

After all these years of learning and tasting I have felt the need to record more than simply the name of a particular whisky along with its nose, taste and flavour. To me, the experience of sampling a dram should allow a clearer picture to be recorded so that, in years to come, I could look back over the many wonderful malts I had tasted and so recall a memory of the day when they first crossed my lips.

This is the purpose of *The Malt Whisky Cellar Book*. I have designed it in such a way that whiskies sourced from high street retailers, independent bottlers, specialist outlets and distilleries themselves can be detailed and recorded as fully as possible, whether they are bought by the bottle or the cask. In this chapter I will take you through the various options open to you if you are about to start on that journey of discovery.

SOURCING MALT WHISKY

Nowadays we are fortunate in having the luxury of being able to walk into a wine shop in just about every town in Britain and choose from a range of fine, bottled single malts; thirty years ago finding a wine shop alone was difficult enough. The situation did not change much in the seventies and it was only in the mid-eighties that wine chains and specialist retailers really began to exploit a growing public interest in malt whisky. Not only can malt whisky be delivered to your door today, you can also check out a number of sites on the Internet and order direct from there (see page 13). More traditional routes are still in existence too. Purchasing direct from a distillery either by the bottle or, more rarely, the cask is still open to you although the latter service is something of an exception to the rule today.

Dealing with a reliable and well-established whisky broker is not really viable because brokers are trade-related and are not in the business of supplying a single cask to a private individual. The best route to go down for that rare and exclusive malt is still your local wine and spirits merchant, specialist whisky shop or an independent bottler, usually by mail order. Companies offering futures in casked whisky stocks should be avoided at all costs; just as the value of your shares portfolio can rise and fall, so too can the value of any stock in bond you might have. If someone guarantees you the value of a cask of malt in ten years time, walk away.

Another alternative is to join a society, club or association specialising in the supply of rare malts. Many of these are well-established and can source very fine vintages from many distilleries. To enable you to find a convenient source I have listed useful addresses and contacts in chapter four.

Some of you might consider collecting bottled malt whiskies, not for drinking, but for 'laying down' as an investment. Whilst I firmly believe that whisky is for drinking and enjoying, I have occasionally regretted not having bought two bottles of a rare vintage in order to keep one for investment purposes. As you will have surmised, even when I was able to do this, temptation got the better of me. But you can make your own judgements: you might come across a bottling from a defunct distillery which is being offered at a keen price, or you could attend one of the regular whisky auctions run by Christie's where, in the space of a day, you will be exposed to more 'whiskyabilia' than you'll come across in a year! Some lots can be bought for fairly reasonable outlays, but do not expect any favours when rare or unique bottlings appear – the bidding is fast and the prices achieved can run into thousands of pounds.

In chapter five I have taken a little time to compile a bibliography in order to further the education of anyone wishing to know more about whisky, its origins, history and development into the world's leading spirit. Regrettably some of these sources are no longer in print, but the ever-widening interest in malt whisky worldwide has created a strong demand for new works on the subject and over the last decade there has been an increase in the number of books published on whisky.

Chapter six deals with those rare and disappearing drams which can be difficult to find. Many of these are from distilleries which are either defunct, mothballed or do not bottle their product commercially. In every case, the chance to purchase a bottle of whisky from these distilleries should not be missed. It is history in a bottle!

Chapter seven contains a number of indexes which have been structured to allow a full understanding of the geographical location of each distillery. The main index consists of all the existing distilleries in Scotland, including the more recently defunct ones, with any associated brand names in brackets. This is followed by regional indexes of distilleries in production or defunct/mothballed. Maps pertaining to these indexes appear on pages 23, 24 and 25.

In order to give a degree of historical perspective on the distilleries which are in existence today, on pages 21 and 22 I have also compiled a list of distilleries which went out of existence at various times during the last two centuries, many of which are still recalled within living memory. Some of them are recognisable even today as former distilleries, such as Annandale at Distillery Farm, near Annan.

It is well to remember that many of these concerns failed due to economic factors of either a local or national nature. Today's distillers have the world to contend with and when the markets of the Far East sneeze, Scotch whisky catches a cold. If there is a memorial today to the Victorian distillers who went bust over a century ago, it is surely the relatively stable state of the industry as we know it. But the names which make up this lengthy list (with which I have not cluttered up the maps) seem to trip off the tongue like a Gaelic lament. More information on these famous names can be found in some of the books I have listed in the bibliography chapter starting on page 14.

That somewhat depressing historical note should not prevent anyone from making the effort to visit a Scottish malt distillery (or even our close neighbours at Old Bushmills in Co Antrim) and in chapter eight there are details of distilleries which welcome visitors. A dram dispensed in its own home always tastes better, believe me.

INDIVIDUAL CELLAR ENTRIES

In Part Two you will find over 110 pages of individual cellar entries for each malt whisky. In the masthead at the top of each page you can record the name of the malt (or brand name if applicable) and the distillery. The legend bar below this allows you to identify the region of production. On the right-hand side, the column entries allow you to record who the supplier was, the relevant sales/distillery contact name and number, date of purchase, price paid on a bottle or cask basis, age when bottled, ABV%, date of distillation, date of bottling, bottle number, cask number and finally, cask type and size.

The left-hand column breaks down into three main areas. The first is the appearance of the malt, followed by the characteristics for nose and taste at full strength. The box below this allows you to record your impressions after the first reduction when an amount of still water has been added. Any other impressions or observations (packaging, filtered/unfiltered, duty-free, export only, limited edition expression and so on) can be recorded in the 'Comments' section along the bottom of the page.

Finally, in order to create a record of page entries of the whiskies you have sampled, on page 145 you will find a self-indexing facility by cellar entry page number with space to record your whiskies. It is unlikely that you will sample all your malts chronologically on an A–Z basis, no matter how well planned your intentions, and so this system will serve as a useful quick reference index.

2

SOME GUIDELINES ON NOSING AND TASTING

The first thing I always tell people who ask me how to go about nosing and tasting malt whisky is 'Be prepared and be in the mood.' So much more pleasure can be extracted from a proper approach to this pastime if a little bit of care is taken before you start.

First, the glass size and shape is everything. I am constantly astonished by the array of glass types in which Scotch has been served to me by people who should know better. The best type of glass should resemble a tulip in shape, have a stem like a wine glass and a volume of around six fluid ounces. The tulip shape allows the aroma of the malt to be captured at the top of the glass as it is nosed. A sherry *copita* is excellent and the Scotch Malt Whisky Society have their own nosing glasses which are ideal. If you have difficulty sourcing something suitable contact Reeves of Edinburgh (see page 12).

Second: always have a white background against which clarity and colour can be evaluated. This can be a tablecloth or a nearby wall.

Third: water. By all means sample neat spirit with a small unreduced sip, but always add water thereafter. Cask strength spirit sends the tastebuds to sleep, sears the palate and induces a vortex of spirit vapour in the nasal passages rendering subjective analysis worthless. Whiskies need water in the same way that flowers do, so keep a supply of still water to hand. Once you have these ingredients, pour a sample which fills the lower part of the bowl of the glass, say about one fluid ounce (28mls). Now we can begin to look at the whisky.

The casual observer might comment that malt whisky is basically a liquid which is normally golden or straw-like in colour, but that is an understatement. The overall colour is an indicator of how the spirit may have matured. Its clarity can tell us the sort of wood in which it has been stored and the way in which it adheres to the side of the glass, after being swirled around the inside, will give an indication as to its strength and fullness of body.

For instance, a pale-yellow, light malt may be the result of a young spirit matured for only a few years, while a richer, deeper sherry-like colour could well indicate that the malt has been matured in an ex-sherry cask for some, or all, of its life. Remember, spirit that is 'new make' (ie just distilled) has the appearance of water, just as gin and vodka do. It is what happens to it after it is put in wood that determines how it will appear in the future. The whisky industry always matures spirit in oak wood and the type of cask used is determined by each producer's wood policy which may require a particular type of cask for a particular spirit. The most common cask is the hogshead of around 250 litres capacity. Other common casks are the American barrel of 180 litres capacity and the butt, of around 500 litres. All of these sizes will have an effect on the maturing whisky in that the smaller the cask, the faster is the maturation time due to the higher ratio of surface area of wood exposed to the volume of whisky contained within.

Degrees of colour will indicate that part, or all, of the maturing period has been spent in Spanish oak or that part, or all, of the whisky has been matured in the same wood. The actual effect of ex-sherry casks is less pronounced than is commonly believed - it is the tight-grained Spanish oak that really imparts colour to a malt. Some distillers are now producing their whiskies by 'double maturing' them firstly in plain oak for a number of years and then using casks of differing sherry types (eg amontillado, oloroso) or even port and Madeira as a means of finishing these distillations off.

Now swirl a sample around the inside of the glass and watch as the spirit falls back down the inside. As the whisky takes to its 'legs' rivulets of spirit congeal on the surface: the 'thicker' the legs, the greater the body of the whisky. The older the whisky, the 'longer' the legs will be, or the greater will be the time taken for the malt to descend the glass.

These then are simple indicators, but they are worthwhile and you should never hurry on to the nosing process without first having undertaken these steps.

NOSING AND TASTING

Without adding water, look for the intensity and complexity of the aroma and the strength of the spirit vapour as you inhale. A cask-strength malt will tend to assault your olfactory senses more vigorously than a standard-strength bottling (40% ABV). If you feel that the spirit vapour is overwhelming your senses, take a break and on returning to the sample, inhale the sample at a slower rate, drawing the aromas into your nostrils in a more gentle manner. This can help you to 'get under' the spirit characteristics and allow the nuances of the other constituents to make themselves more apparent.

Next, add some water. How much? A good maxim is as much again as the strength of the whisky. In other words, if it is 40% ABV cut it with a volume of 40% water; a 60% ABV malt needs a 60% volume of water. Now, after this 'first reduction' nose the whisky again. The water will have opened the malt creating a much more accessible bouquet to allow the complexities of the whisky to be investigated.

Now taste some of the whisky. Allow a small amount to lie in the 'cup' of your tongue, then raise it against the roof of your mouth and press slowly so that the spirit washes around your tongue. Hold it here for a moment and then swallow slowly. In so doing, the malt will have come into contact with the main sensory areas of taste and allowed you to detect influences of saltiness, sweetness, sourness and bitterness.

At this stage the primary descriptors detected on the nose can be further defined by actually identifying what you are experiencing in taste terms. I cover this in more detail in the next chapter. After tasting the whisky, set it aside for a few minutes to allow it to develop. If you have a cap for the glass, place it over it. On returning to the sample, remove the cap and nose the sample again. You may note that descriptors not apparent at the first nosing of the reduced sample are now coming through. Similarly, another taste may reveal alterations to the flavour of the sample.

MOUTHFEEL

This really deals with the way the whisky feels against the walls and roof of your mouth. Your tongue will detect all the essential flavour descriptors, along with elements of prickle and sharpness, but the reaction of your sensory apparatus within the rest of your mouth will allow you to determine whether the sample is smooth or coarse, whether it is full-, medium- or light-bodied and the malt's relative viscosity. Some malts have a tendency to exert a cloying, or fatty characteristic, but this may not be unpleasant. Always allow a whisky to linger a while to establish its mouthfeel characteristics.

THE FINISH

When you have swallowed the whisky, try to determine the length of its finish. Some whiskies have astonishingly long finishes which are still on the palate hours (and sometimes a good night's sleep) later, while others drift off the palate in a matter of moments. However, it is not true to say that the most pungent and robust of malts will exert the longest finishes – some of the lighter, more floral and estery drams can display astonishingly long finishes. But if there is a guideline here, it is the longer the maturation, the longer the finish.

It is also a good idea to leave enough room when making individual entries to recap on your impressions a little later, perhaps even the next day, when you may be exposed to an aroma, or recall one which immediately brings to mind a nuance which you were unable to pinpoint the first time round. The brain has an incredible ability to recall odours and smells and the memory of an aroma once sensed and seemingly forgotten can lie dormant until awakened by an innocent trigger, so don't underestimate your ability to describe a whisky!

IN SUMMARY

In closing this brief chapter I must impress upon you that there is no shame attached to sensing a component in a whisky which none of the published connoisseurs have attributed to it. Nosing and tasting malt whisky is a *subjective* pleasure which, if allowed free rein (notwithstanding the boundaries of your bank manager's generosity!) can grow into something of an obsession. The only impressions that should matter to you when making your entries are your own ones.

3

THE LANGUAGE OF SCOTCH

In order to understand what you are tasting in a malt, you first need to sample a reasonable number of them and form your own opinions before analysing in greater depth the structure of each one. Beginners should not be subjected to an expert's analysis, which may overwhelm them with information; better that they induct themselves to detect the overall style of a malt's bouquet, mouthfeel, intensity of flavour and its complexity.

Always be honest with yourself in dealing with what you are sensing. If you detect chocolate or cocoa in a whisky's bouquet, then jot down that particular impression. I recall just such a sensation emanating from some of the Bowmore malts I have nosed. It was not there on the palate, and I was ribbed mercilessly for my opinion by a fellow connoisseur, but that is what I detected and so that is what I recorded. Few experts will arrive at an identical conclusion after sampling the same whisky so there is nothing to be ashamed of.

Some pointers can be helpful with regard to detecting styles and characteristics which are due to regional influences. Although there can be exceptions to these generalities, they will help in identifying a particular whisky's area of production.

SPEYSIDE: the sweetest malts and frequently accompanied with floral overtones and honey notes.

HIGHLANDS: this area encompasses the country surrounding Speyside on all points of the compass. In general the northern malts are delicate and aromatic, the eastern malts are often fuller-bodied and dry with slightly smoky overtones while the southern malts from around Perthshire are 'quick' whiskies (lacking long finishes) and are fruity in nature though not as sweet as the Speysides. The western Highland malts are few in number and are heavier in nature than the other Highland malts, expressing a degree of peatiness with some sweet notes.

LOWLANDS: generally light, aromatic and estery although some vintage bottlings do belie these characteristics.

ISLANDS: generally peaty-smoky and sweet though not as robust as the Islays.

ISLAY: peaty-smokey with sea salt in the south and floral overtones in the west. Robust, sweet and full-bodied in the south.

CAMPBELTOWN: heavier than the Lowlands with hints of Islay, the sea and Ireland.

Science can, however, tell us a great deal about the origins of what we are actually nosing and tasting, but each person will detect varying influences to a greater or lesser degree. Here are some basic guidelines to the characteristics that might be detected in a malt. I am indebted to Dr Jim Swan and my colleague and fellow connoisseur Charles MacLean who have burned a great deal of midnight oil in developing the concept of the 'whisky wheel' as an aid for the trade and enthusiast alike. I have drawn on their considerable research to outline the language that I hope will add a little objectivity to descriptive terms.

PRIMARY AROMATIC CHARACTERISTICS will be immediately recognisable at the nosing stage such as the degree of peatiness or the intensity of influence from Spanish oak ex-sherry casks which can add sherry overtones. These characteristics can be defined under eight main headings: CEREAL, FRUITY, FLORAL, PEATY, FEINTY, SULPHURY, WOODY and WINEY. All of these can be examined further upon actual tasting.

For instance, CEREAL characteristics might be described as cooked, mashed vegetables, malt extract, bran and porridge. You may even detect hops or sweetcorn. FRUITY derivatives might be peel zest, pineapple, pear drops, boiled sweets, fruit cake and sultanas.

FLORAL attributes can fall under lavender, grass cuttings, sage, dry hay or heather and PEATINESS may be reflected in medicinal overtones such as TCP, iodine or lint or in seashore terms such as dried shellfish, anchovies or smoked oysters and also in any degree of smokiness which might reveal itself.

FEINTY characteristics can be detected in less attractive terms and you may detect plastic, oilskin, shoe polish, sweet tobacco, leather and beeswax.

SULPHUR terms might include decaying vegetation such as cabbage water, marsh gas and brackish water while rubbery influences are commonly described, such as new tyres and pencil erasers.

WOODINESS is obviously a characteristic associated with maturation and it is no surprise that many tasters detect vanilla flavours within this descriptor. New wood flavours can remind one of cigar boxes and nutmeg whereas old wood characteristics can resemble cardboard or cork. Frequently, toasted flavours are detected such as bread crust or burnt toast.

Finally the WINEY flavours encompass hock, chardonnay, oloroso and fino sherry and a detectable nuttiness might manifest itself with walnuts, praline and almonds. Chocolate overtones are discernible with cream, cocoa and bitter chocolate.

By utilising these main descriptive terms you should more readily be able to tackle the broad range of whiskies in a systematic, but nonetheless subjective way.

4

USEFUL ADDRESSES AND CONTACTS

Gone are the days when the search for a particular bottle of malt meant a stream of phone calls around the country or a journey to a distant specialist retailer. Even if you have access only to the 'high street', a visit to Oddbins will probably be the answer. However, there are some sources with access to vintage and rare malt whiskies who can be very helpful when trying to find that elusive spirit. The companies/retailers and websites listed in this chapter are worth contacting if only to review their latest bottling lists and to see if they have any special offers available. I have listed them alphabetically by country and indicated if they are independent bottlers, societies, clubs or retailers.

One of the best ways to appreciate the sheer variety of malt whisky available today is to join a club or society. Foremost amongst these are the Scotch Malt Whisky Society in Leith and the Whisky Connoisseur Club based in Biggar. Some distillers have set up their own clubs such as Friends of Laphroaig, Still Friends of Glenfarclas and Friends of the Classic Malts. Membership of these consumer societies can be gained by contacting them directly or responding to the distiller's point-of-sale instructions when purchasing a bottle of the relevant malt. Frequently, a visit to any of the distilleries in question will lead to the same result. There are a number of benefits to joining these clubs or societies, not least of which are product news and invitations to events and tastings. Some specialist retailers such as Loch Fyne Whiskies in Inveraray publish their own informative newsletter which is sent out regularly to their trade customers. More significantly, *Whisky Magazine* (see page 14) is a major source of information and is essential to anyone with a passion for malt whisky.

The whisky trade is a very consumer-friendly business which is always open to approaches from the general public so feel free to contact as many of the organisations listed here as you see fit.

SCOTLAND

INDEPENDENT BOTTLERS

Adelphi Distillery
3 Gloucester Lane
EDINBURGH EH3 6ED
t: 0131-226-6670
f: 0131-226-6672
Contact: Bryn Whalley
w: http://www.highlandtrail.co.uk/spirit2.html

Blackadder International
Logie Green
LARKHALL
Lanarkshire ML9 1DA
t: 01435-883309
Contact: John Lamond

Cadenheads Whisky Shop
172 Canongate
EDINBURGH EH8 8BN
t: 0131-556-5864
f: 0131-556-2527
(retail and mixed cases)
t: 01586-554258 (wholesale)
Contact: Craig Clapperton

Gordon & MacPhail Ltd
George House
Boroughbriggs Road
ELGIN, Morayshire IV30 1JY
t: 01343-545111
f: 01343-540155
Contact: Marketing department

Hart Brothers (1988) Ltd
85 Springkell Avenue
GLASGOW G41 4EJ
t: 0141-427-6974
f: 0141-427-9300
Contact: Alastair or Donald Hart

Signatory Vintage Scotch Whisky Co Ltd
7/8 Elizafield
Newhaven Road
EDINBURGH EH6 5PY
t: 0131-555-4988
f: 0131-555-5211
Contact: Andrew Symington

The Vintage Malt Whisky Co
2 Stewart Street
MILNGAVIE G62 6BW
t: 0141-955-1700
f: 0141-955-1701
Contact: Brian Crook
w: http://www.vintage-malt whisky.co.uk

SPECIALIST RETAILERS

Aberdeen Whisky Shop
c/o Hector Russell Kiltmaker
409 Union Street
ABERDEEN AB1 2DA
t: 01224-581584

Cairngorm Whisky Centre
Inverdruie, AVIEMORE
Inverness-shire PH22 1QH
t&f: 01479-810574
Contact: Frank Clark

Callander Whisky Shop
11 Main Street, CALLANDER
Perthshire FK17 8DU
t: 01887-331936

Drumnadrochit Whisky Shop
The Official Loch Ness Monster Exhibition
DRUMNADROCHIT
Inverness-shire IV3 6TU
t&f: 01456-450321

Eaglesome Ltd
Reform Square
CAMPBELTOWN
Argyllshire PA28 6JA
t: 01586-551710

Edinburgh Whisky Shop
Unit L2B, Waverley Market
Princes Street
EDINBURGH EH1 1BQ
t: 0131-556-5688

Fort William Whisky Shop
93 High Street
FORT WILLIAM
Inverness-shire PH33 6DH
t: 01397-706164

Glasgow Whisky Shop
Unit 12, Princes Square
48 Buchanan Street
GLASGOW G1 3JN
t: 0141-226-8446

Inverness Whisky Shop
17 Bridge Street
INVERNESS IV1 1HD
t: 01463-710525

Loch Fyne Whiskies
INVERARAY, Argyll PA32 8UD
t: 01499-302219
f: 01499-302238
w: http://www.lfw.co.uk
Contact: Richard Joynson

Luvian's Bottle Shop
93 Bonnygate
CUPAR, Fife KY15 4LG
t&f: 01334-654820
Contact: Vince Fusaro

Moffat Wine Shop
8 Well Street
MOFFAT
Dumfriesshire DG10 9DP
t: 01683- 220554
Contact: Tony McIlwrick

Oban Whisky Shop
112 George Street
OBAN, Argyllshire PA34 5NT
t: 01631-564409

Princes Street Whisky Shop
96 Princes Street
EDINBURGH EH2 2ER
t: 0131-220-5899

Royal Mile Whiskies
379 High Street
EDINBURGH EH1 1PW
t: 0131-225-3383
f: 0131-226-2772

Strachan's of Aboyne
Balmoral Terrace
ABOYNE
Aberdeenshire AB34 5HL
t: 01339-886121

The Ubiquitous Chip
Wine Shop
12 Ashton Lane
Byres Road
GLASGOW G2 8SJ
t: 0141-334-7109

The Whisky Castle
Main Street
TOMINTOUL
AB37 9EX
t: 01807-580-213

The Whisky Shop
Buchanan Galleries
GLASGOW G1 2GF
t: 0141-331-0022

SOCIETIES/CLUBS

Friends of the Classic Malts
PO BOX 87
GLASGOW G14 0JF
t: 0141-300-4900
f: 0141-300-4949

Friends of Laphroaig
Laphroaig Distillery
PORT ELLEN
Islay PA42 7DU
t: 01496-302418
f: 01496-302496
Contact: Iain Henderson

Friends of Tranquillity
The Glenmorangie Distillery Coy
FREEPOST 478
TAIN, Ross-shire IV19 1BR

Scotch Malt Whisky Society
The Vaults, 87 Giles Street
LEITH EH6 6BZ
t: 0131-554-3451
f: 0131-553-1003
w: http://www.smws.co.uk

Scotch Whisky Heritage Centre
354 Castlehill
EDINBURGH EH6 6BZ
t: 0131-220-0441

Still Friends of Glenfarclas
FREEPOST SCO 3715
EAST KILBRIDE G74 1BR

The Whisky Connoisseur
Thistle Mill
BIGGAR
Lanarkshire ML12 6LP
t: 01899-221001

AUCTIONEERS

Christie's Scotland
164 Bath Street
GLASGOW G2 4TB
t: 0141-332-8134
f: 0141-332-5759

GLASS SUPPLIERS

W Reeves & Co
40 Potterow
EDINBURGH EH8 9BT
t: 0131-667-9225
f: 0131-662-4908

ENGLAND

INDEPENDENT BOTTLERS

Murray McDavid
56 Walton Street
LONDON SW3 1RB
t: 0171-823-7717
f: 0171-581-0250
Contact: Gordon Wright

John Milroy
Independent Whisky Purveyor
Top Suite, 3 Greek Street, Soho
LONDON W1V 5LA
t: 0171-287-4985
f: 0171-287-4985
Contact: John Milroy

SPECIALIST RETAILERS

Cadenheads Whisky Shop
3 Russell Street
Covent Garden
LONDON WC2B 5JD
t: 0171-379-46404
f: 0171-379-4600
Contact: Sean Ivers

Milroys of Soho
3 Greek Street, Soho
LONDON W1V 6NX
t: 0171-437-0893
f: 0171-437-1345
Contact: Doug McIvor, Bridget Arthur

Fortnum & Mason
181 Piccadilly
LONDON W1A ER
t: 0171-734-8040
f: 0171-437-3278
Contact: Annette Duce

Harrods Ltd
Knightsbridge
LONDON SW1X 7XL
t: 0171-730-1234, ext 3162
f: 0171-225-5823
Contact: Alistair Viner

Selfridges Ltd
400 Oxford Street
LONDON W1A 1AB
t: 0171-318-3730
f: 0171-491-1880
Contact: Colin Akers

The Nest
106/108 Uxbridge Road
Hanwell
LONDON W7 3SU
t: 0181-579-7273
f: 0181-840-9431
Contact: Sukindar Singh

The Vintage House
42 Old Compton Street, Soho
LONDON W1V 6LR
t: 0171-437-2592
f: 0171-734-1174
w: http://www.vintagehouse.co.uk
Contact: Michael Mullin
or Michael Barton

The Wright Wine Company
The Old Smithy, Raikes Road
SKIPTON
North Yorkshire BD23 1NP
t: 01756-700886
f: 01756-798580
Contact: Julian Kaye

Tanner's Wines
26 Wyle Cop
SHREWSBURY
Shropshire SY1 1XD
t: 01743-234455
f: 01743-234501
Contact: John Melhuish

SOCIETIES/CLUBS

The Malt Whisky Association
96A Calverley Road
TUNBRIDGE WELLS
Kent TN1 2UN
t: 01892-513295

The Whisky Club
PO BOX 43
SHREWSBURY
Shropshire SY2 5WU
t: 01743-249999
Contact: Peter Hebblethwaite

INTERNET WEBSITES

Generic sites

http://www.islaywhisky.com
http://www.scotchwhisky.com
http://www.scotch-whisky.org.uk
(Scotch Whisky Association)
http://www.whiskeypages.com
(Malt Advocate Magazine)
http://whiskymag.com
(The Whisky Magazine)
http://www.whiskyweb.com

Retailers

http://www.gordonandmacphail.co.uk
http://www.lfw.co.uk
(Loch Fyne Whiskies, Scotland)

http://www.smws.com
(Scotch Malt Whisky Society)
http://www.vintagehouse.co.uk
http://www.whiskyshop.com
(The Whisky Shop, Scotland)

Malts

http://www.ardbeg.com
http://www.bladnoch.co.uk
http://www.glenfiddich.com
http://www.glengoyne.com
http://www.glenmorangie.com
http://www.glenmoray.com
http://www.glenord.com
http://www.glenturret.com
http://www.highlandpark.co.uk
http://www.laphroaig.com
http://www.thebalvenie.com
http://www.theglenlivet.com
http://www.themacallan-themalt.com

Blends

http://www.ballantines.com
http://www.blackbottle.com
http://www.buchanans.com
http://www.cattos.com
http://www.chivas.com
http://www.cutty-sark.com
http://www.dewars.co.uk
http://www.famousgrouse.com
http://www.hankeybannister.com

Whisky Liqueurs

http://www.drambuie.com
http://www.wallace-malt.co.uk

Corporate and Company

http://www.ianmacleod.com
http://www.defmalt.com
http://www.inverhouse.com
http://www.morrisonbowmore.co.uk
http://www.scotch.com
(United Distillers & Vintners)
http://www.speysidedistillery.co.uk

Whisky Links Site

http://home.swipnet.se/whisky/

5

BIBLIOGRAPHY AND USEFUL SOURCES

Of whisky and golf it seems, there can never be enough books. In my case, my bookshelves groan only with those of the former subject although both are perhaps Scotland's greatest contributions to modern-day living. In order to create a useful list of references, I have chosen sources for their availability. The first section deals with books which can still be bought in a bookshop or specialist outlet. The second contains details of books and sources now confined to the catalogues of antiquarian booksellers, reference libraries and company archives.

A number of privately-published sources are in existence but I have ignored these in order to concentrate on those sources which can be found and accessed with relative ease.

Of perhaps more immediate interest to whisky drinkers is the recent establishment of *The Whisky Magazine*, (*t:* 0181-563-2975) the first issue of which was published in November 1998. This is a welcome development and I recommend taking out a subscription to it.

SOURCES WIDELY AVAILABLE

Arthur, Helen, *The Single Malt Whisky Companion*, Apple, 1997
Single Malt Whisky, Apple Identifier, 1998
Brown, Gordon, *The Whisky Trails*, Prion, 1993
Bruce Lockhart, Sir Robert, *Scotch, The Whisky of Scotland in Fact and Story*, NWP, 1995
Burns, Edward, *Bad Whisky*, Balvag Books, 1995
Cooper, Derek, *A Taste of Scotch*, André Deutsch, 1989
Daiches, David, *Scotch Whisky: Its Past and Present*, Birlinn, 1995
Jackson, Michael, *The Malt Whisky Companion*, Dorling Kindersley, 1994
The World Guide To Whisky, Dorling Kindersley, 1987
Gabányi, Stefan, *Whisk(e)y*, Abbeville, 1997
Greenwood, Malcolm, *A Nip Around The World*, Argyll, 1995
Another Nip Around The World, NWP, 1996

Gray, Alan, *The Scotch Whisky Industry Review*, published annually

Hills, Philip (ed), *Scots on Scotch*, Mainstream, 1991

McDowall, RJS, *The Whiskies of Scotland*, John Murray, 1986

MacLean, Charles, *Malt Whisky*, Mitchell Beazley, 1997

Scotch Whisky, Mitchell Beazley Pocket Guides, 1998

An Introduction to Malt Whisky, J Sainsbury plc, 1995

Martine, Roddy, *Scotland: The Land and The Whisky*, Keepers of the Quaich, 1994

McIvor, Douglas. *Scotch Whisky: Top Single Malts*, PRC, 1998

Milroy, Wallace, *The Original Malt Whisky Almanac*, (7th ed) NWP, 1998

Moore, Graham, *Malt Whisky: A Contemporary Guide*, Swanhill, 1998

Murray, Jim, *Classic Irish Whiskey*, Prion, 1997

Complete Book of Whisky, Carlton, 1997

Nown, Graham, *Malt Whisky*, Salamander, 1997

Shaw, Carol, *Whisky*, Collins Gem Series, 1993

Smith, Gavin D, *A-Z of Whisky*, NWP, 1998

Storrie, Margaret, *Islay: Biography of an Island*, Oa Press, 1998

Townsend, Brian, *Scotch Missed: The Lost Distilleries of Scotland*, NWP, 1997

The Lost Distilleries of Ireland, NWP, 1997

Tucek, Robin and Lamond, John, *The Malt Whisky File*, (2nd ed) Canongate, 1997

Whisky Magazine, published every two months since November 1998

Wilson, Neil, *Scotch and Water: An Illustrated Guide to the Hebridean Malt Whisky Distilleries*, NWP, 1998

SOURCES CURRENTLY OUT OF PRINT

Andrews, Allen, *The Whisky Barons*, Jupiter Books, 1977

Barnard, Alfred, *The Whisky Distilleries of the United Kingdom*, Harper's Weekly Gazette, 1887

Barnard, Alfred, *The Whisky Distilleries of the United Kingdom*, Centenary Edition, Mainstream/Lochar, 1987

Cooper, Derek & Godwin, Fay, *The Whisky Roads of Scotland*, Jill Norman & Hobhouse, 1982

Craig, Charles, *The Scotch Whisky Industry Record*, Index, 1994

Dunnett, Sir Alastair, *Land of Scotch*, SWA, 1953

Gunn, Neil, *Whisky and Scotland*, Souvenir, 1998

Morewood, Samuel, *A Philosophical and Statistical History of the Inventions and Customs of Ancient and Modern Nations in the Manufacture of Inebriating Liquors*, Dublin, 1838

Morrice, Philip, *The Schweppes Guide to Scotch*, Alphabooks, 1983

Moss, Michael & Hume, John, *The Making of Scotch Whisky*, James & James, 1981

Nettleton, JA, *The Manufacture of Spirit as Conducted at the Various Distilleries of the United Kingdom*, G Cornwall & Sons, 1913

Smith, Gavin D, *Whisky: A Book of Words*, Carcanet, 1993

Weir, Ronald, *The History of the Distillers Company, 1877-1939*, Clarendon, 1995

Wilson, Ross, *Scotch Made Easy*, Hutchinson, 1959

Wilson, Ross, *Scotch: The Formative Years*, Constable, 1970

Wilson, Ross, *Scotch: Its History and Romance*, David & Charles, 1973

6

RARE AND VINTAGE MALTS

The portfolio of rare malts available on the market at any one time is an organic one. Frequently a search for a malt distilled in the 1940s or 50s will meet with no success and even the most diligent collector ends up admitting defeat. Then, as though by magic, a distiller or independent bottler 'discovers' a rare cache consisting of a few forgotten barrels deep in the dark recesses of a gloomy bond. True, a real 'find' does come to light from time to time, but I prefer to think that today's whisky trade recognises the commercial value of a rare malt knowing full well that when those few hundred bottles are released, an asking price of a couple of hundred pounds or more will not be regarded as unrealistic.

The moral of this is a simple one…don't give up. Some unbelievable bottlings have emerged at regular whisky auctions and been snapped up by voracious collectors. As to whether or not they have then been opened and sampled is most unlikely; it seems that very few of the bidders at these auctions allow themselves that pleasure. For myself, I believe firmly that whisky is the water of life and as such should be drunk, not kept in a gilded cage as a conversation piece.

This list consists of malt whiskies which are now considered rare in that they seldom find their way on to the market and are well worth acquiring. Some are from distilleries either defunct, mothballed or simply non-existent; others, remarkably, are from distilleries which exist but whose owners do not market these malts such as Braeval and Strathmill.

Some of the malts do not carry the name of the distillery which produced them, so take note of the fact that Glen Flagler was distilled at Moffat Distillery, which is nowhere near Moffat in Dumfriesshire, but was once part of the distilling complex owned by Inver House near Airdrie in Lanarkshire!

Obviously, there will be rare vintages from well-known distilleries which are in production and become available from time to time so keep a sharp eye out for limited-release trade expressions.

Speyside

Allt-a'Bhainne, nr Dufftown
1975-. In production. Available through the independent bottlers.

Braeval, nr Tomintoul
In production. Formerly known as Braes of Glenlivet. Available through the independent bottlers.

Coleburn, Elgin
1897-1985. Still standing.

Convalmore, Dufftown
1894-1985. Now owned by Wm Grant & Sons. No plans to reopen.

Dallas Dhu, Forres
1899-. Distilling ceased in 1983. Exists as a museum.

Glen Elgin, Elgin
*c*1900-. In production. A crack whisky which rarely finds its way into the bottle.

Glen Spey, Rothes
1878-. In production. Very rare.

Strathmill, Keith
1891-. In production. Very rare.

Highland (Northern)

Brora (or Old Clynelish), Brora
1819-1983. Still standing with reinstatement not planned.

Glen Albyn, Inverness
1846-1986. Demolished.

Glen Mhor, Inverness
1892-1986. Demolished.

Millburn, Inverness
1807-1988. Demolished.

Highland (Eastern)

Banff, Banff
1863-1983. Demolished.

Glenugie, Peterhead
1831-1983.
Part-converted/demolished.

Glenury-Royal, Stonehaven
1825-1985. Redeveloped.

Hillside or North Esk, Montrose
1897-. Permanently mothballed, *aka* Glenesk.

Lochside, Montrose
1957-1991. Due for demolition/redevelopment.

North Port, Brechin
1820-1983. Demolished 1994.

Highland (Western)

Glenlochy, Fort William
1898-1983. Pagoda and some associated buildings still standing.

Lowlands

Clydesdale, Wishaw
1825-1919. Demolished 1988.

Inverleven, Dumbarton
1938-1991. Permanently mothballed, *aka* Lomond.

Kinclaith, Glasgow
1957-1975. Dismantled.

Ladyburn, Girvan
1966-. Ceased distilling in 1975.

Moffat, Airdrie
1968-1985. Dismantled, *aka* Glen Flagler and Killyloch.

St Magdalene, Linlithgow
1798-1983. Part-converted to accommodation.

Islay

Port Ellen, Port Ellen
1825-1983. Still standing. Will probably never reopen.

Campbeltown

Glen Scotia
1832-. Mothballed 1994. May reopen in due course. Difficult to find.

Longrow
1828-. Rarely available.

7

INDEXES

DISTILLERIES WITH ASSOCIATED BRAND NAMES

Distilleries are listed along with any associated names (in brackets). Maps pertaining to these distilleries appear on pages 23, 24 and 25. This list includes mothballed, recently defunct and some 'lost' distilleries of which the odd bottle can still be found, such as Kinclaith.

DISTILLERIES CURRENTLY IN PRODUCTION BY REGION

These distilleries are currently in production or producing sporadically, notwithstanding annual maintenance shutdowns.

MOTHBALLED DISTILLERIES BY REGION

These distilleries do not produce whisky, and the dates given refer to the year of establishment and year of closure. Some have only recently been 'mothballed' and so their prospects are not as poor as those which have been consigned to 'defunct' status as listed on page 21.

RECENTLY DEFUNCT DISTILLERIES BY REGION

Many of the distilleries listed here have been demolished or adapted for other purposes within living memory. It is generally accepted that the defunct distilleries which are still standing have no prospect of ever distilling again and are therefore as good as 'lost', such as Parkmore.

LOST DISTILLERIES BY REGION

Almost without exception, these distilleries simply do not exist intact any more; most of them having had their heyday in the mid to late 19th century. The list is not comprehensive, but covers some of the better documented plants about which more than simply basic information still exists. Occasionally a bottle from one of these long-lost distilleries does turn up. In November 1990 a 40-year-old Dalintober from Campbeltown was auctioned at Christie's, Glasgow, fetching £2530. The malt had been distilled in 1868 and bottled in 1908!

Aberfeldy
Aberlour
Allt-a'Bhainne
Ardbeg
Ardmore
Auchentoshan
Auchroisk *(The Singleton of Auchroisk)*
Aultmore
Balblair
Balmenach
Balvenie
Banff
Ben Nevis
Benriach
Benrinnes
Benromach
Bladnoch
Blair Athol
Bowmore
Braeval
Brora or Old Clynelish
Bruichladdich *(Lochindaal)*
Bunnahabhain
Caol Ila
Caperdonich
Cardhu
Clydesdale
Clynelish
Coleburn
Convalmore
Cragganmore
Craigellachie
Dailuaine
Dallas Dhu
Dalmore
Dalwhinnie
Deanston
Dufftown
Edradour
Fettercairn *(Old Fettercairn)*
Glen Albyn
Glen Elgin
Glen Garioch
Glen Grant
Glen Keith
Glen Mhor
Glen Moray
Glen Ord
Glen Scotia
Glen Spey
Glenallachie
Glenburgie *(Glencraig)*
Glencadam
Glendronach
Glendullan
Glenfarclas
Glenfiddich
Glenglassaugh
Glengoyne
Glenkinchie
Glenlivet
Glenlochy
Glenlossie
Glenmorangie
Glenrothes
Glentauchers
Glenturret
Glenugie
Glenury-Royal
Highland Park
Hillside or North Esk *(Glenesk)*
Imperial
Inchgower
Inverleven *(Lomond)*
Isle of Jura
Kinclaith
Kininvie
Knockando
Knockdhu *(An Cnoc)*
Ladyburn
Lagavulin
Laphroaig
Linkwood
Littlemill
Loch Lomond *(Inchmurrin, Old Rhosdhu)*
Lochranza *(Isle of Arran)*
Lochside
Longmorn
Macallan
Macduff *(Glen Deveron)*
Mannochmore *(Loch Dhu)*
Millburn
Miltonduff *(Mosstowie)*
Moffat *(Glen Flagler, Killyloch)*
Mortlach
North Port
Oban
Old Bushmills
Parkmore
Pittyvaich
Port Ellen
Pulteney *(Old Pulteney)*
Rosebank
Royal Brackla
Royal Lochnagar
Scapa
Speyburn
Speyside *(Drumguish)*
Springbank *(Longrow)*
St Magdalene
Strathisla
Strathmill
Talisker
Tamdhu
Tamnavulin
Teaninich
Tobermory *(Ledaig)*
Tomatin
Tomintoul
Tormore
Tullibardine

DISTILLERIES CURRENTLY IN PRODUCTION BY REGION

Speyside

Aberlour
Ardmore
Allt-a'Bhainne
Auchroisk
Aultmore
Balmenach
Balvenie
Benriach
Benrinnes
Benromach
Braeval
Caperdonich
Cardhu
Cragganmore
Craigellachie
Dailuaine
Dufftown
Glen Elgin
Glen Grant
Glen Keith
Glen Moray
Glen Spey
Glenallachie
Glenburgie
Glendullan
Glenfarclas
Glenfiddich
Glenlivet
Glenlossie
Glenrothes
Glentauchers
Inchgower
Kininvie
Knockando
Knockdhu
Linkwood
Longmorn
Macallan
Mannochmore
Miltonduff
Mortlach
Speyburn
Strathisla
Strathmill
Tamdhu
Tomintoul
Tormore

Highland (Northern)

Balblair
Clynelish
Dalmore
Dalwhinnie
Glen Ord
Glenmorangie
Pulteney
Royal Brackla
Speyside
Teaninich
Tomatin

Highland (Eastern)

Glen Garioch
Glencadam
Fettercairn
Macduff
Royal Lochnagar

Highland (Western)

Ben Nevis
Oban

Highland (Southern)

Aberfeldy
Blair Athol
Deanston
Edradour
Glengoyne
Glenturret
Loch Lomond

Lowland

Auchentoshan
Glenkinchie

Islay

Ardbeg
Bowmore
Bruichladdich
Bunnahabhain
Caol Ila
Lagavulin
Laphroaig

Campbeltown

Springbank

Island

Highland Park
Isle of Jura
Lochranza
Talisker
Tobermory

Northern Ireland

Old Bushmills

Ireland (not on maps)

Cooley
Midleton

MOTHBALLED DISTILLERIES BY REGION

Speyside

Dallas Dhu
1899–1983

Glendronach
1826–1998

Glenglassaugh
1875–1998

Imperial
1897–1998

Pittyvaich
1974–. Intermittently operational.

Tamnavulin
1965–1995

Highland (Southern)

Tullibardine
1949–1995

Lowland

Bladnoch
1817–1993

Littlemill
1772–1992

Rosebank
1840–1993

Islay

Port Ellen
1825–1983

Campbeltown

Glen Scotia
1832–1994

Island (Orkney)

Scapa
1824–1994

RECENTLY DEFUNCT DISTILLERIES BY REGION

Speyside

Coleburn
1897–1985

Convalmore
1894–1985

Parkmore
1894–1931

Highland (Northern)

Brora (or Old Clynelish)
1819–1983

Glen Albyn
1846–1983

Glen Mhor
1892–1983

Millburn
1807–1985

Highland (Eastern)

Banff
1863–1983

Glenugie
1831–1983

Glenury-Royal
1826–1986

Hillside or North Esk
1897–1985

Lochside
1957–1991

North Port
1820–1983

Highland (Western)

Glenlochy
1898–1983

Lowland

Clydesdale
1825–1919

Inverleven
1938–1991

Kinclaith
1957–1975

Ladyburn
1966–1975

Moffat
1968–1985

St Magdalene
1798–1983

LOST DISTILLERIES BY REGION

Highland (Northern)

Ben Wyvis, Dingwall
1879–1926

Gerston, Halkirk
1798–1882

Gerston II, Halkirk
1886–1911

Glen Cawdor, Nairn
1898–1927

Glenskiath, Evanton
1896–1926

Pollo, Delny
1817–1903

Speyside, Kingussie
1895–1911

Highland (Eastern)

Auchinblae, Kincardine
1896–1926

Banff, Inverboyndie
1863–1983

Benachie, Insch
1822–1915

Bon Accord, Aberdeen
1822-1910
Devanha, Aberdeen
1827-1915
Glencoull, Justinhaugh
1897-1929
Glenaden, Old Deer
1882-1915
Strathdee, Aberdeen
1821-c1945
Towiemore, Botriphnie
1896-1930

Highland (Western)

Glendarroch, Ardrishaig
1831-1937
Nevis, Fort William
1878-1908

Highland (Southern)

Auchnagie, Tulliemet
1827-1912
Ballechin, Ballinluig
1810-1927
Glenfoyle, Gargunnock
1795-1923
Grandtully, Aberfeldy
1825-1910
Isla, Perth
1851-1926
Stronachie, Forgandenny
1900-1928

Lowland

Adelphi, Glasgow
1825-1907
Annandale, Annan
1830-1921
Auchtermuchty, Fife
1829-1926
Auchtertool, Fife
1845-1927
Bankier, Stirlingshire
1827-1928
Bo'ness, West Lothian
1813-1925
Camlachie, Glasgow
1834-1920
Dean, Edinburgh
1881-1922
Dundashill, Glasgow
1770-1903
Glenpatrick, Elderslie
1833-1894
Glen Sciennes
Edinburgh
1849-1925
Glen Tarras, Langholm
1839-1915
Greenock, Geenock
1795-1915
Langholm, Langholm
1765-1921
Provanmill, Glasgow
1815-1929
Tambowie, Milngavie
1825-1910

Islay

Lochindaal,
Port Charlotte
1829-1929

Campbeltown

Albyn, The Roading
1830-1927
Ardlussa, Glebe St
1879-1923
Argyll, Longrow
1844-1923
Benmore, Saddell St
1868-1927
Burnside, Witchburn Rd
1825-1924
Campbeltown, Longrow
1817-1924
Dalaruan, Broad St
1824-1922
Dalintober, Queen St
1832-1925
Glengyle, Glengyle Rd
1873-1925
Glen Nevis, Glebe St
1877-1923
Glenside, Glenside
1834-1926
Hazelburn, Longrow
1825-1925
Kinloch, Longrow
1823-1926
Kintyre, Broad St
1825-1921
Lochhead, Lochend
1824-1928
Lochruan, Princes St
1835-1925
Longrow, off Longrow
1824-1896
Meadowburn, Tomaig Rd
1824-1886
Rieclachan, off Longrow
1825-1934
Springside, Burnside St
1830-1926

Island (Orkney)

Man o'Hoy, Stromness
1817-1928

KEY
ISLANDS
Towns
Distilleries
ORKNEY
Kirkwall
Highland Park
Thurso
Wick
Pulteney
LEWIS
Clynelish
Brora
Ullapool
Dornoch
N. UIST
HARRIS
Balblair
Invergordon
Glenmorangie
Teaninich
Elgin
Dingwall
Dalmore
Macduff
Nairn
Glen Ord
Portree
Inverness
Royal Brackla
SPEYSIDE
(see separate map)
Peterhead
Talisker
Kyle of Lochalsh
Glen Garioch
S. UIST
SKYE
Speyside
Kingussie
Aberdeen
Mallaig
BARRA
RHUM
Royal Lochnagar
Fort William
Dalwhinnie
Ben Nevis
Fettercairn
COLL
Glencadam
Tobermory
Edradour
Brechin
Pitlochry
Blair Athol
Montrose
Aberfeldy
Forfar
TIREE
Oban
MULL
Dundee
Arbroath
Oban
Glenturret
Perth
Deanston
JURA
Stirling
Kirkcaldy
Bunnahabhain
Loch Lomond
Glengoyne
Caol Ila
Auchentoshan
ISLAY
Isle of Jura
Greenock
Glasgow
Edinburgh
Bruichladdich
Glenkinchie
Bowmore
Port Ellen
Lochranza
Ardbeg
Laphroaig
ARRAN
Kilmarnock
Lagavulin
Ayr
Springbank
Old Bushmills
Dumfries
NORTHERN IRELAND
Newton Stewart
Belfast

SPEYSIDE DISTILLERIES IN PRODUCTION

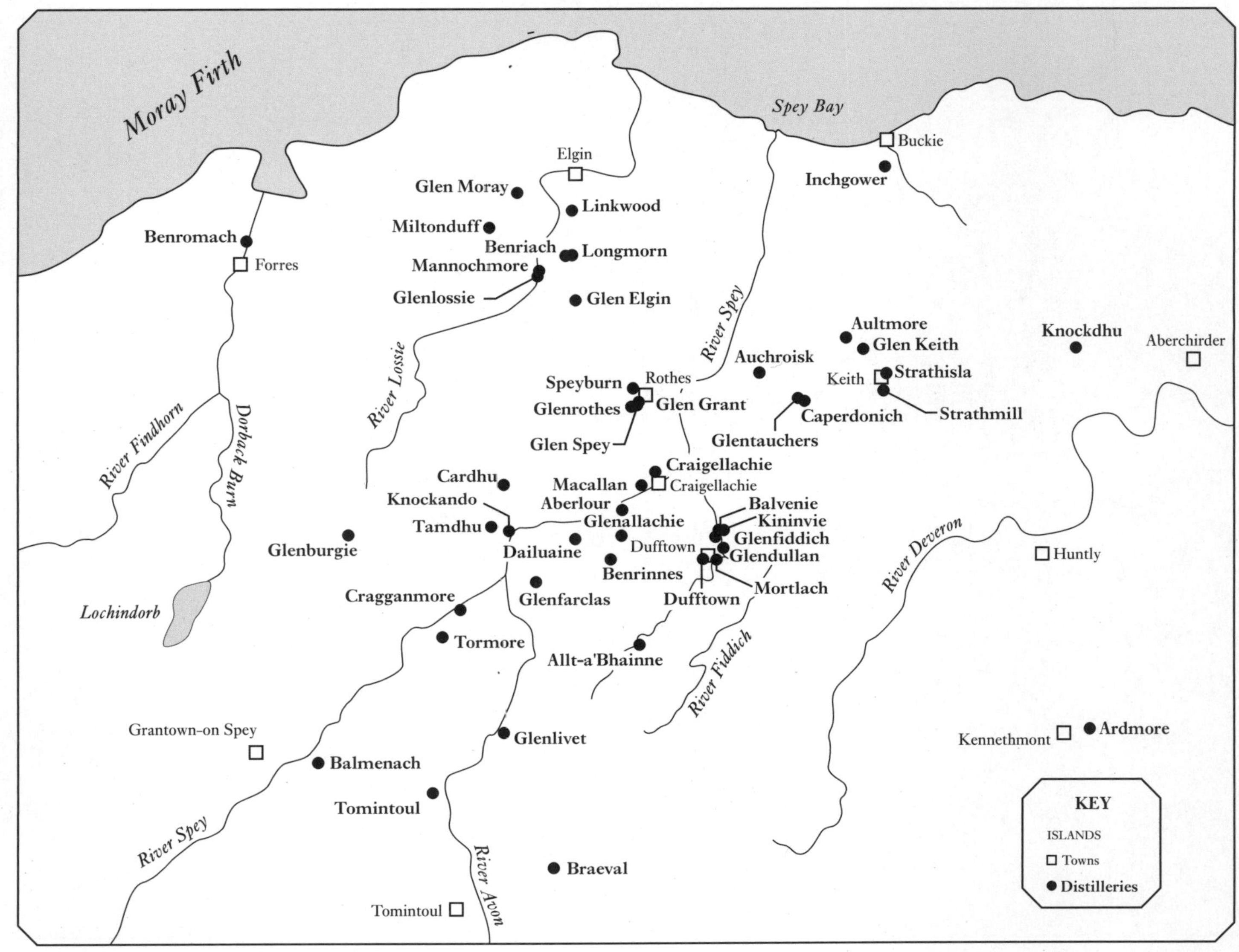

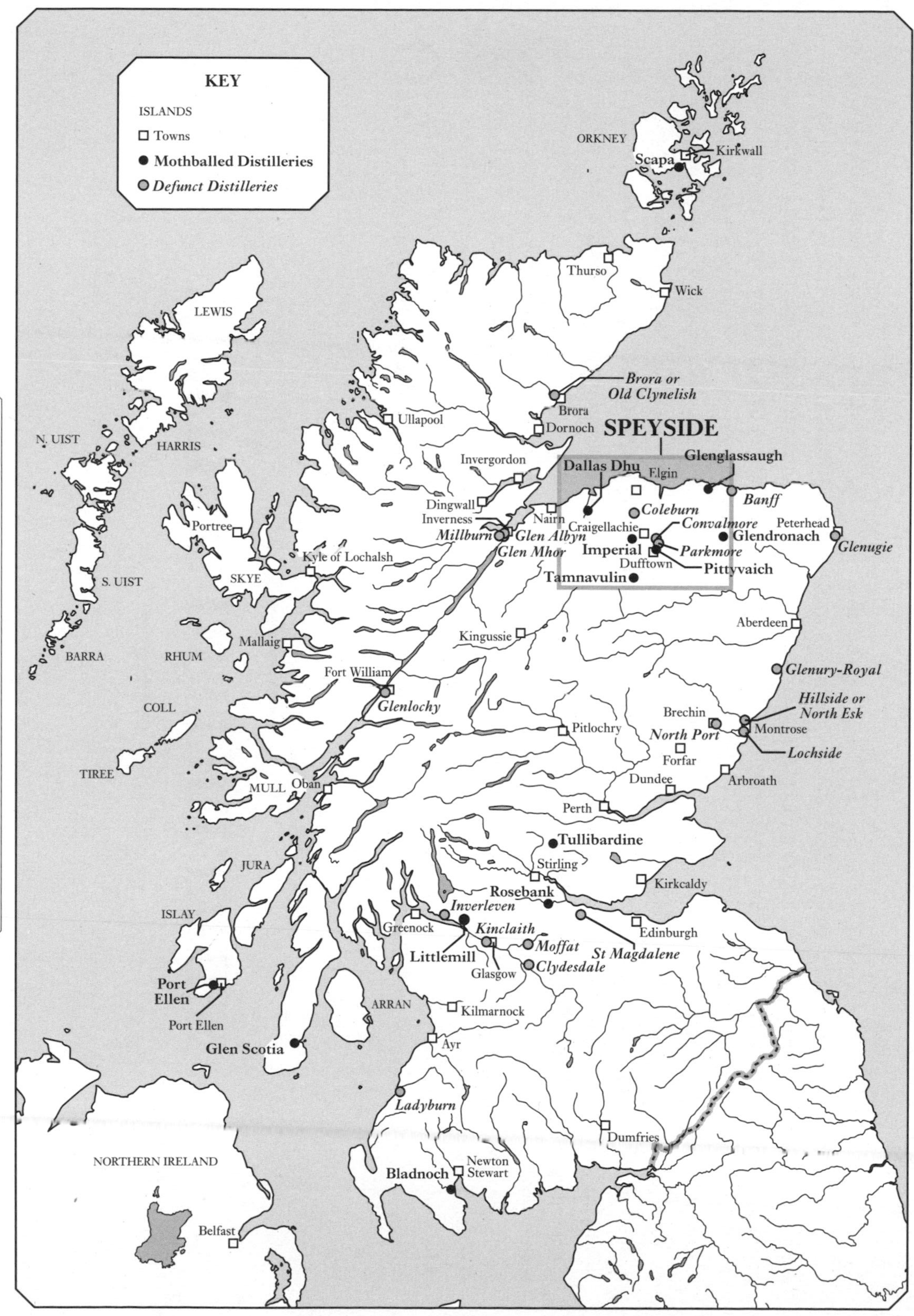
KEY
ISLANDS
Towns
Mothballed Distilleries
Defunct Distilleries
ORKNEY
Scapa
Kirkwall
Thurso
Wick
LEWIS
Brora or Old Clynelish
Brora
Dornoch
Ullapool
N. UIST
HARRIS
SPEYSIDE
Invergordon
Dallas Dhu
Elgin
Glenglassaugh
Dingwall
Inverness
Nairn
Coleburn
Banff
Portree
Craigellachie
Convalmore
Peterhead
Millburn
Glen Albyn
Glen Mhor
Imperial
Parkmore
Glendronach
Glenugie
Kyle of Lochalsh
Dufftown
Pittyvaich
SKYE
S. UIST
Tamnavulin
Aberdeen
Mallaig
Kingussie
BARRA
RHUM
Fort William
Glenury-Royal
Glenlochy
COLL
Brechin
Hillside or North Esk
Montrose
Pitlochry
North Port
Lochside
Forfar
TIREE
Dundee
Arbroath
MULL
Oban
Perth
Tullibardine
Stirling
JURA
Kirkcaldy
Rosebank
Inverleven
ISLAY
Greenock
Kinclaith
Edinburgh
Moffat
Littlemill
St Magdalene
Glasgow
Clydesdale
Port Ellen
Port Ellen
ARRAN
Kilmarnock
Glen Scotia
Ayr
Ladyburn
Dumfries
NORTHERN IRELAND
Newton Stewart
Bladnoch
Belfast

8

VISITING DISTILLERIES

One of the great pleasures of whisky tasting is to sample a malt at the distillery where it is produced. If you have had the good fortune to travel in Speyside or to visit Islay the whisky seems to convey the very essence of its locality. Whisky is literally made on the seashore in the islands and so many of these fine whiskies betray that close association.

Over the last ten years the industry has begun to take distillery tourism seriously and the result is an ever-increasing number of places where the complete malt experience can be gained. The list on the next two pages is compiled from distilleries currently offering some sort of reception facility from the all-consuming tour, tasting and shopping experience to the simple 'pleased to see you, I'll show you around' attitude which you will find at many of the more remote distilleries. Wherever you find yourself, the experience of a visit to a distillery is worth all the effort in getting there.

For those wanting someone else to undertake the sometimes horrendous logistics of a trip around some of Scotland's distilleries, there is a new company willing to arrange flexible packages to suit every pocket. Distillery Destinations (see page 28) can undertake whisky tours (amongst other whisky-related activities) and help you avoid the pitfalls many find themselves in, such as trying to do the impossible.

I recall one American visitor telling me he intended driving from Glasgow to Campbeltown in the morning with stops at Auchentoshan and Springbank before heading 'through the glens' via Oban to be in Speyside late in the afternoon. He even asked me if I thought he would have time for a bite to eat in Oban!

But if you are going to do it yourself, one final word of advice: always telephone in advance to make sure the distillery expects you and if you are running late, always try to let them know. Enjoy!

Speyside

Cardhu*
ABERLOUR
BANFFSHIRE AB38 7RY
t: 01340-810204

Dallas Dhu*
FORRES
MORAYSHIRE IV36 0RR
t: 01309-676548

Glen Grant*
ROTHES
MORAYSHIRE AB38 7BS
t: 01542-783318

Glen Keith
KEITH
BANFFSHIRE AB55 3BU
t: 01542-783044

Glenfarclas*
BALLINDALLOCH
BANFFSHIRE AB37 9BD
t: 01807-500257

Glenfiddich*
DUFFTOWN
BANFFSHIRE AB55 4DH
t: 01340-820373

Knockando
ABERLOUR
MORAYSHIRE AB38 7RD
t: 01340-810205

Longmorn
ELGIN
MORAYSHIRE IV30 3SJ
t: 01542-783042

Strathisla*
KEITH
BANFFSHIRE AB55 3BS
t: 01542-783044

Glendronach
HUNTLY
ABERDEENSHIRE AB54 6DB
t: 01466-730202

Glenlivet*
BALLINDALLOCH
BANFFSHIRE AB37 9DB
t: 01542-783220

Macallan
ABERLOUR
BANFFSHIRE AB38 9RX
t: 01340-871471

Tamnavulin
BALLINDALLOCH
BANFFSHIRE AB37 9JA
t: 01807-590442

**Denotes distilleries on the Speyside Malt Whisky Trail*

Highland (Northern)

Clynelish
BRORA
SUTHERLAND KW9 6LR
t: 01408-623014

Dalwhinnie
DALWHINNIE
INVERNESS-SHIRE PH19 1AB
t: 01528-522208

Glen Ord
MUIR OF ORD
ROSS-SHIRE IV6 7UJ
t: 01463-872004

Glenmorangie
TAIN
ROSS-SHIRE IV19 1PZ
t: 01862-892477

Tomatin
TOMATIN
INVERNESS-SHIRE IV13 7YT
t: 01808-511444

Highland (Eastern)

Old Fettercairn
LAURENCEKIRK
KINCARDINESHIRE AB30 1YE
t: 01561-340244

Royal Lochnagar
BALLATER
ABERDEENSHIRE AB35 5TB
t: 01339-742273

Highland (Western)

Ben Nevis
FORT WILLIAM
INVERNESS-SHIRE PH33 6TJ
t: 01397-700200

Oban
OBAN
ARGYLL PA34 5NH
t: 01631-572004

Highland (Southern)

Aberfeldy
ABERFELDY
PERTHSHIRE PH15 2EB
t: 01887-820330

Blair Athol
PITLOCHRY
PERTHSHIRE PH16 5LY
t: 01360-550254

Glengoyne
DUMGOYNE
STIRLINGSHIRE G63 9LB
t: 01360-550254

Edradour
PITLOCHRY
PERTHSHIRE PH16 5JP
t: 01796-472095

Glenturret
CRIEFF
PERTHSHIRE PH7 4HA
t: 01764-656565

Lowlands

Bladnoch
BLADNOCH
WIGTOWNSHIRE DG8 9AB
t: 01988-402605

Glenkinchie
PENCAITLAND
EAST LOTHIAN EH34 5ET
t: 01875-342002

Islay

Ardbeg
ISLAY
ARGYLL PA42 7DU
t: 01496-302244

Bowmore
ISLAY
ARGYLL PA43 7JS
t: 01496-810441

Bunnahabhain
ISLAY
ARGYLL PA46 7RP
t: 01496-840646

Caol Ila
ISLAY
ARGYLL PA46 7RL
t: 01496-840207

Lagavulin
ISLAY
ARGYLL PA42 7DZ
t: 01496-302217

Laphroaig
ISLAY
ARGYLL PA42 7DU
t: 01496-302418

Islands

Highland Park
KIRKWALL
ORKNEY KW15 1SU
t: 01856-874619

Isle of Arran
LOCHRANZA
ISLE OF ARRAN
ARGYLL KA27 8HJ
t: 01770-830264

Talisker
CARBOST
ISLE OF SKYE IV47 8SR
t: 01478-640314

Tobermory
ISLE OF MULL
ARGYLL PA75 6NR
t: 01688-302647

Northern Ireland

Old Bushmills
BUSHMILLS
CO ANTRIM BT57 8XH
t: 012657-31521

SPECIALIST TRAVEL COMPANIES

Distillery Destinations
304 ALBERT DRIVE
GLASGOW G41 5RS
t: 0141-429-0762

PART TWO

CELLAR ENTRIES

MALT

DISTILLERY

SPEYSIDE ☐ HIGHLAND NORTHERN ☐ HIGHLAND EASTERN ☐ HIGHLAND WESTERN ☐ HIGHLAND SOUTHERN ☐ LOWLAND ☐ ISLAY ☐ ISLANDS ☐ CAMPBELTOWN ☐ IRELAND ☐ OTHER ☐

APPEARANCE

FULL STRENGTH

NOSE

TASTE

FIRST REDUCTION

NOSE

TASTE

SUPPLIED BY

CONTACT NAME/NUMBER

DATE OF PURCHASE

PRICE PAID – BOTTLE CASK

AGE WHEN BOTTLED

BOTTLED ABV %

DATE OF DISTILLATION

DATE OF BOTTLING

BOTTLE NUMBER CASK NUMBER

CASK TYPE CASK SIZE

COMMENTS

MALT

DISTILLERY

SPEYSIDE ☐ HIGHLAND NORTHERN ☐ HIGHLAND EASTERN ☐ HIGHLAND WESTERN ☐ HIGHLAND SOUTHERN ☐ LOWLAND ☐ ISLAY ☐ ISLANDS ☐ CAMPBELTOWN ☐ IRELAND ☐ OTHER ☐

APPEARANCE

FULL STRENGTH

NOSE

TASTE

FIRST REDUCTION

NOSE

TASTE

SUPPLIED BY

CONTACT NAME/NUMBER

DATE OF PURCHASE

PRICE PAID – BOTTLE CASK

AGE WHEN BOTTLED

BOTTLED ABV %

DATE OF DISTILLATION

DATE OF BOTTLING

BOTTLE NUMBER CASK NUMBER

CASK TYPE CASK SIZE

COMMENTS

MALT

DISTILLERY

SPEYSIDE ☐ HIGHLAND NORTHERN ☐ HIGHLAND EASTERN ☐ HIGHLAND WESTERN ☐ HIGHLAND SOUTHERN ☐ LOWLAND ☐ ISLAY ☐ ISLANDS ☐ CAMPBELTOWN ☐ IRELAND ☐ OTHER ☐

APPEARANCE

FULL STRENGTH

NOSE

TASTE

FIRST REDUCTION

NOSE

TASTE

SUPPLIED BY

CONTACT NAME/NUMBER

DATE OF PURCHASE

PRICE PAID – BOTTLE CASK

AGE WHEN BOTTLED

BOTTLED ABV %

DATE OF DISTILLATION

DATE OF BOTTLING

BOTTLE NUMBER CASK NUMBER

CASK TYPE CASK SIZE

COMMENTS

MALT

DISTILLERY

SPEYSIDE ☐ HIGHLAND NORTHERN ☐ HIGHLAND EASTERN ☐ HIGHLAND WESTERN ☐ HIGHLAND SOUTHERN ☐ LOWLAND ☐ ISLAY ☐ ISLANDS ☐ CAMPBELTOWN ☐ IRELAND ☐ OTHER ☐

APPEARANCE

FULL STRENGTH

NOSE

TASTE

FIRST REDUCTION

NOSE

TASTE

SUPPLIED BY

CONTACT NAME/NUMBER

DATE OF PURCHASE

PRICE PAID – BOTTLE CASK

AGE WHEN BOTTLED

BOTTLED ABV %

DATE OF DISTILLATION

DATE OF BOTTLING

BOTTLE NUMBER CASK NUMBER

CASK TYPE CASK SIZE

COMMENTS

MALT

DISTILLERY

SPEYSIDE ☐ HIGHLAND NORTHERN ☐ HIGHLAND EASTERN ☐ HIGHLAND WESTERN ☐ HIGHLAND SOUTHERN ☐ LOWLAND ☐ ISLAY ☐ ISLANDS ☐ CAMPBELTOWN ☐ IRELAND ☐ OTHER ☐

APPEARANCE

FULL STRENGTH

NOSE

TASTE

FIRST REDUCTION

NOSE

TASTE

SUPPLIED BY

CONTACT NAME/NUMBER

DATE OF PURCHASE

PRICE PAID – BOTTLE CASK

AGE WHEN BOTTLED

BOTTLED ABV %

DATE OF DISTILLATION

DATE OF BOTTLING

BOTTLE NUMBER CASK NUMBER

CASK TYPE CASK SIZE

COMMENTS

MALT

DISTILLERY

SPEYSIDE ☐ HIGHLAND NORTHERN ☐ HIGHLAND EASTERN ☐ HIGHLAND WESTERN ☐ HIGHLAND SOUTHERN ☐ LOWLAND ☐ ISLAY ☐ ISLANDS ☐ CAMPBELTOWN ☐ IRELAND ☐ OTHER ☐

APPEARANCE

FULL STRENGTH

NOSE

TASTE

FIRST REDUCTION

NOSE

TASTE

SUPPLIED BY

CONTACT NAME/NUMBER

DATE OF PURCHASE

PRICE PAID – BOTTLE CASK

AGE WHEN BOTTLED

BOTTLED ABV %

DATE OF DISTILLATION

DATE OF BOTTLING

BOTTLE NUMBER CASK NUMBER

CASK TYPE CASK SIZE

COMMENTS

MALT

DISTILLERY

SPEYSIDE ☐ HIGHLAND NORTHERN ☐ HIGHLAND EASTERN ☐ HIGHLAND WESTERN ☐ HIGHLAND SOUTHERN ☐ LOWLAND ☐ ISLAY ☐ ISLANDS ☐ CAMPBELTOWN ☐ IRELAND ☐ OTHER ☐

APPEARANCE

FULL STRENGTH

NOSE

TASTE

FIRST REDUCTION

NOSE

TASTE

SUPPLIED BY

CONTACT NAME/NUMBER

DATE OF PURCHASE

PRICE PAID – BOTTLE CASK

AGE WHEN BOTTLED

BOTTLED ABV %

DATE OF DISTILLATION

DATE OF BOTTLING

BOTTLE NUMBER CASK NUMBER

CASK TYPE CASK SIZE

COMMENTS

MALT

DISTILLERY

SPEYSIDE ☐ HIGHLAND NORTHERN ☐ HIGHLAND EASTERN ☐ HIGHLAND WESTERN ☐ HIGHLAND SOUTHERN ☐ LOWLAND ☐ ISLAY ☐ ISLANDS ☐ CAMPBELTOWN ☐ IRELAND ☐ OTHER ☐

APPEARANCE

FULL STRENGTH

NOSE

TASTE

FIRST REDUCTION

NOSE

TASTE

SUPPLIED BY

CONTACT NAME/NUMBER

DATE OF PURCHASE

PRICE PAID – BOTTLE CASK

AGE WHEN BOTTLED

BOTTLED ABV %

DATE OF DISTILLATION

DATE OF BOTTLING

BOTTLE NUMBER CASK NUMBER

CASK TYPE CASK SIZE

COMMENTS

MALT

DISTILLERY

SPEYSIDE ☐ HIGHLAND NORTHERN ☐ HIGHLAND EASTERN ☐ HIGHLAND WESTERN ☐ HIGHLAND SOUTHERN ☐ LOWLAND ☐ ISLAY ☐ ISLANDS ☐ CAMPBELTOWN ☐ IRELAND ☐ OTHER ☐

APPEARANCE

FULL STRENGTH

NOSE

TASTE

FIRST REDUCTION

NOSE

TASTE

SUPPLIED BY

CONTACT NAME/NUMBER

DATE OF PURCHASE

PRICE PAID – BOTTLE CASK

AGE WHEN BOTTLED

BOTTLED ABV %

DATE OF DISTILLATION

DATE OF BOTTLING

BOTTLE NUMBER CASK NUMBER

CASK TYPE CASK SIZE

COMMENTS

MALT

DISTILLERY

SPEYSIDE ☐ HIGHLAND NORTHERN ☐ HIGHLAND EASTERN ☐ HIGHLAND WESTERN ☐ HIGHLAND SOUTHERN ☐ LOWLAND ☐ ISLAY ☐ ISLANDS ☐ CAMPBELTOWN ☐ IRELAND ☐ OTHER ☐

APPEARANCE

FULL STRENGTH

NOSE

TASTE

FIRST REDUCTION

NOSE

TASTE

SUPPLIED BY

CONTACT NAME/NUMBER

DATE OF PURCHASE

PRICE PAID – BOTTLE CASK

AGE WHEN BOTTLED

BOTTLED ABV %

DATE OF DISTILLATION

DATE OF BOTTLING

BOTTLE NUMBER CASK NUMBER

CASK TYPE CASK SIZE

COMMENTS

MALT

DISTILLERY

SPEYSIDE ☐ HIGHLAND NORTHERN ☐ HIGHLAND EASTERN ☐ HIGHLAND WESTERN ☐ HIGHLAND SOUTHERN ☐ LOWLAND ☐ ISLAY ☐ ISLANDS ☐ CAMPBELTOWN ☐ IRELAND ☐ OTHER ☐

APPEARANCE

FULL STRENGTH

NOSE

TASTE

FIRST REDUCTION

NOSE

TASTE

SUPPLIED BY

CONTACT NAME/NUMBER

DATE OF PURCHASE

PRICE PAID – BOTTLE CASK

AGE WHEN BOTTLED

BOTTLED ABV %

DATE OF DISTILLATION

DATE OF BOTTLING

BOTTLE NUMBER CASK NUMBER

CASK TYPE CASK SIZE

COMMENTS

MALT

DISTILLERY

SPEYSIDE ☐ HIGHLAND NORTHERN ☐ HIGHLAND EASTERN ☐ HIGHLAND WESTERN ☐ HIGHLAND SOUTHERN ☐ LOWLAND ☐ ISLAY ☐ ISLANDS ☐ CAMPBELTOWN ☐ IRELAND ☐ OTHER ☐

APPEARANCE

FULL STRENGTH

NOSE

TASTE

FIRST REDUCTION

NOSE

TASTE

SUPPLIED BY

CONTACT NAME/NUMBER

DATE OF PURCHASE

PRICE PAID – BOTTLE CASK

AGE WHEN BOTTLED

BOTTLED ABV %

DATE OF DISTILLATION

DATE OF BOTTLING

BOTTLE NUMBER CASK NUMBER

CASK TYPE CASK SIZE

COMMENTS

MALT

DISTILLERY

SPEYSIDE ☐ HIGHLAND NORTHERN ☐ HIGHLAND EASTERN ☐ HIGHLAND WESTERN ☐ HIGHLAND SOUTHERN ☐ LOWLAND ☐ ISLAY ☐ ISLANDS ☐ CAMPBELTOWN ☐ IRELAND ☐ OTHER ☐

APPEARANCE

FULL STRENGTH

NOSE

TASTE

FIRST REDUCTION

NOSE

TASTE

SUPPLIED BY

CONTACT NAME/NUMBER

DATE OF PURCHASE

PRICE PAID – BOTTLE CASK

AGE WHEN BOTTLED

BOTTLED ABV %

DATE OF DISTILLATION

DATE OF BOTTLING

BOTTLE NUMBER CASK NUMBER

CASK TYPE CASK SIZE

COMMENTS

MALT

DISTILLERY

SPEYSIDE ☐ HIGHLAND NORTHERN ☐ HIGHLAND EASTERN ☐ HIGHLAND WESTERN ☐ HIGHLAND SOUTHERN ☐ LOWLAND ☐ ISLAY ☐ ISLANDS ☐ CAMPBELTOWN ☐ IRELAND ☐ OTHER ☐

APPEARANCE

FULL STRENGTH

NOSE

TASTE

FIRST REDUCTION

NOSE

TASTE

SUPPLIED BY

CONTACT NAME/NUMBER

DATE OF PURCHASE

PRICE PAID – BOTTLE CASK

AGE WHEN BOTTLED

BOTTLED ABV %

DATE OF DISTILLATION

DATE OF BOTTLING

BOTTLE NUMBER CASK NUMBER

CASK TYPE CASK SIZE

COMMENTS

MALT

DISTILLERY

SPEYSIDE ☐ HIGHLAND NORTHERN ☐ HIGHLAND EASTERN ☐ HIGHLAND WESTERN ☐ HIGHLAND SOUTHERN ☐ LOWLAND ☐ ISLAY ☐ ISLANDS ☐ CAMPBELTOWN ☐ IRELAND ☐ OTHER ☐

APPEARANCE

FULL STRENGTH

NOSE

TASTE

FIRST REDUCTION

NOSE

TASTE

SUPPLIED BY

CONTACT NAME/NUMBER

DATE OF PURCHASE

PRICE PAID – BOTTLE CASK

AGE WHEN BOTTLED

BOTTLED ABV %

DATE OF DISTILLATION

DATE OF BOTTLING

BOTTLE NUMBER CASK NUMBER

CASK TYPE CASK SIZE

COMMENTS

MALT

DISTILLERY

SPEYSIDE ☐ HIGHLAND NORTHERN ☐ HIGHLAND EASTERN ☐ HIGHLAND WESTERN ☐ HIGHLAND SOUTHERN ☐ LOWLAND ☐ ISLAY ☐ ISLANDS ☐ CAMPBELTOWN ☐ IRELAND ☐ OTHER ☐

APPEARANCE

FULL STRENGTH

NOSE

TASTE

FIRST REDUCTION

NOSE

TASTE

SUPPLIED BY

CONTACT NAME/NUMBER

DATE OF PURCHASE

PRICE PAID – BOTTLE CASK

AGE WHEN BOTTLED

BOTTLED ABV %

DATE OF DISTILLATION

DATE OF BOTTLING

BOTTLE NUMBER CASK NUMBER

CASK TYPE CASK SIZE

COMMENTS

MALT

DISTILLERY

SPEYSIDE ☐ HIGHLAND NORTHERN ☐ HIGHLAND EASTERN ☐ HIGHLAND WESTERN ☐ HIGHLAND SOUTHERN ☐ LOWLAND ☐ ISLAY ☐ ISLANDS ☐ CAMPBELTOWN ☐ IRELAND ☐ OTHER ☐

APPEARANCE

FULL STRENGTH

NOSE

TASTE

FIRST REDUCTION

NOSE

TASTE

SUPPLIED BY

CONTACT NAME/NUMBER

DATE OF PURCHASE

PRICE PAID – BOTTLE CASK

AGE WHEN BOTTLED

BOTTLED ABV %

DATE OF DISTILLATION

DATE OF BOTTLING

BOTTLE NUMBER CASK NUMBER

CASK TYPE CASK SIZE

COMMENTS

MALT

DISTILLERY

SPEYSIDE ☐ HIGHLAND NORTHERN ☐ HIGHLAND EASTERN ☐ HIGHLAND WESTERN ☐ HIGHLAND SOUTHERN ☐ LOWLAND ☐ ISLAY ☐ ISLANDS ☐ CAMPBELTOWN ☐ IRELAND ☐ OTHER ☐

APPEARANCE

FULL STRENGTH

NOSE

TASTE

FIRST REDUCTION

NOSE

TASTE

SUPPLIED BY

CONTACT NAME/NUMBER

DATE OF PURCHASE

PRICE PAID – BOTTLE CASK

AGE WHEN BOTTLED

BOTTLED ABV %

DATE OF DISTILLATION

DATE OF BOTTLING

BOTTLE NUMBER CASK NUMBER

CASK TYPE CASK SIZE

COMMENTS

MALT

DISTILLERY

SPEYSIDE ☐ HIGHLAND NORTHERN ☐ HIGHLAND EASTERN ☐ HIGHLAND WESTERN ☐ HIGHLAND SOUTHERN ☐ LOWLAND ☐ ISLAY ☐ ISLANDS ☐ CAMPBELTOWN ☐ IRELAND ☐ OTHER ☐

APPEARANCE

FULL STRENGTH

NOSE

TASTE

FIRST REDUCTION

NOSE

TASTE

SUPPLIED BY

CONTACT NAME/NUMBER

DATE OF PURCHASE

PRICE PAID – BOTTLE CASK

AGE WHEN BOTTLED

BOTTLED ABV %

DATE OF DISTILLATION

DATE OF BOTTLING

BOTTLE NUMBER CASK NUMBER

CASK TYPE CASK SIZE

COMMENTS

MALT

DISTILLERY

SPEYSIDE ☐ HIGHLAND NORTHERN ☐ HIGHLAND EASTERN ☐ HIGHLAND WESTERN ☐ HIGHLAND SOUTHERN ☐ LOWLAND ☐ ISLAY ☐ ISLANDS ☐ CAMPBELTOWN ☐ IRELAND ☐ OTHER ☐

APPEARANCE

FULL STRENGTH

NOSE

TASTE

FIRST REDUCTION

NOSE

TASTE

SUPPLIED BY

CONTACT NAME/NUMBER

DATE OF PURCHASE

PRICE PAID – BOTTLE CASK

AGE WHEN BOTTLED

BOTTLED ABV %

DATE OF DISTILLATION

DATE OF BOTTLING

BOTTLE NUMBER CASK NUMBER

CASK TYPE CASK SIZE

COMMENTS

MALT

DISTILLERY

SPEYSIDE ☐ HIGHLAND NORTHERN ☐ HIGHLAND EASTERN ☐ HIGHLAND WESTERN ☐ HIGHLAND SOUTHERN ☐ LOWLAND ☐ ISLAY ☐ ISLANDS ☐ CAMPBELTOWN ☐ IRELAND ☐ OTHER ☐

APPEARANCE

FULL STRENGTH

NOSE

TASTE

FIRST REDUCTION

NOSE

TASTE

SUPPLIED BY

CONTACT NAME/NUMBER

DATE OF PURCHASE

PRICE PAID – BOTTLE CASK

AGE WHEN BOTTLED

BOTTLED ABV %

DATE OF DISTILLATION

DATE OF BOTTLING

BOTTLE NUMBER CASK NUMBER

CASK TYPE CASK SIZE

COMMENTS

MALT

DISTILLERY

SPEYSIDE ☐ HIGHLAND NORTHERN ☐ HIGHLAND EASTERN ☐ HIGHLAND WESTERN ☐ HIGHLAND SOUTHERN ☐ LOWLAND ☐ ISLAY ☐ ISLANDS ☐ CAMPBELTOWN ☐ IRELAND ☐ OTHER ☐

APPEARANCE

FULL STRENGTH

NOSE

TASTE

FIRST REDUCTION

NOSE

TASTE

SUPPLIED BY

CONTACT NAME/NUMBER

DATE OF PURCHASE

PRICE PAID – BOTTLE CASK

AGE WHEN BOTTLED

BOTTLED ABV %

DATE OF DISTILLATION

DATE OF BOTTLING

BOTTLE NUMBER CASK NUMBER

CASK TYPE CASK SIZE

COMMENTS

MALT

DISTILLERY

SPEYSIDE ☐ HIGHLAND NORTHERN ☐ HIGHLAND EASTERN ☐ HIGHLAND WESTERN ☐ HIGHLAND SOUTHERN ☐ LOWLAND ☐ ISLAY ☐ ISLANDS ☐ CAMPBELTOWN ☐ IRELAND ☐ OTHER ☐

APPEARANCE

FULL STRENGTH

NOSE

TASTE

FIRST REDUCTION

NOSE

TASTE

SUPPLIED BY

CONTACT NAME/NUMBER

DATE OF PURCHASE

PRICE PAID – BOTTLE CASK

AGE WHEN BOTTLED

BOTTLED ABV %

DATE OF DISTILLATION

DATE OF BOTTLING

BOTTLE NUMBER CASK NUMBER

CASK TYPE CASK SIZE

COMMENTS

MALT

DISTILLERY

SPEYSIDE ☐ HIGHLAND NORTHERN ☐ HIGHLAND EASTERN ☐ HIGHLAND WESTERN ☐ HIGHLAND SOUTHERN ☐ LOWLAND ☐ ISLAY ☐ ISLANDS ☐ CAMPBELTOWN ☐ IRELAND ☐ OTHER ☐

APPEARANCE

FULL STRENGTH

NOSE

TASTE

FIRST REDUCTION

NOSE

TASTE

SUPPLIED BY

CONTACT NAME/NUMBER

DATE OF PURCHASE

PRICE PAID – BOTTLE CASK

AGE WHEN BOTTLED

BOTTLED ABV %

DATE OF DISTILLATION

DATE OF BOTTLING

BOTTLE NUMBER CASK NUMBER

CASK TYPE CASK SIZE

COMMENTS

MALT

DISTILLERY

SPEYSIDE ☐ HIGHLAND NORTHERN ☐ HIGHLAND EASTERN ☐ HIGHLAND WESTERN ☐ HIGHLAND SOUTHERN ☐ LOWLAND ☐ ISLAY ☐ ISLANDS ☐ CAMPBELTOWN ☐ IRELAND ☐ OTHER ☐

APPEARANCE

FULL STRENGTH

NOSE

TASTE

FIRST REDUCTION

NOSE

TASTE

SUPPLIED BY

CONTACT NAME/NUMBER

DATE OF PURCHASE

PRICE PAID – BOTTLE CASK

AGE WHEN BOTTLED

BOTTLED ABV %

DATE OF DISTILLATION

DATE OF BOTTLING

BOTTLE NUMBER CASK NUMBER

CASK TYPE CASK SIZE

COMMENTS

MALT DISTILLERY

SPEYSIDE ☐ HIGHLAND NORTHERN ☐ HIGHLAND EASTERN ☐ HIGHLAND WESTERN ☐ HIGHLAND SOUTHERN ☐ LOWLAND ☐ ISLAY ☐ ISLANDS ☐ CAMPBELTOWN ☐ IRELAND ☐ OTHER ☐

APPEARANCE

FULL STRENGTH

NOSE

TASTE

FIRST REDUCTION

NOSE

TASTE

SUPPLIED BY

CONTACT NAME/NUMBER

DATE OF PURCHASE

PRICE PAID – BOTTLE CASK

AGE WHEN BOTTLED

BOTTLED ABV %

DATE OF DISTILLATION

DATE OF BOTTLING

BOTTLE NUMBER CASK NUMBER

CASK TYPE CASK SIZE

COMMENTS

MALT

DISTILLERY

SPEYSIDE ☐ HIGHLAND NORTHERN ☐ HIGHLAND EASTERN ☐ HIGHLAND WESTERN ☐ HIGHLAND SOUTHERN ☐ LOWLAND ☐ ISLAY ☐ ISLANDS ☐ CAMPBELTOWN ☐ IRELAND ☐ OTHER ☐

APPEARANCE

FULL STRENGTH

NOSE

TASTE

FIRST REDUCTION

NOSE

TASTE

SUPPLIED BY

CONTACT NAME/NUMBER

DATE OF PURCHASE

PRICE PAID – BOTTLE CASK

AGE WHEN BOTTLED

BOTTLED ABV %

DATE OF DISTILLATION

DATE OF BOTTLING

BOTTLE NUMBER CASK NUMBER

CASK TYPE CASK SIZE

COMMENTS

MALT

DISTILLERY

SPEYSIDE ☐ HIGHLAND NORTHERN ☐ HIGHLAND EASTERN ☐ HIGHLAND WESTERN ☐ HIGHLAND SOUTHERN ☐ LOWLAND ☐ ISLAY ☐ ISLANDS ☐ CAMPBELTOWN ☐ IRELAND ☐ OTHER ☐

APPEARANCE

FULL STRENGTH

NOSE

TASTE

FIRST REDUCTION

NOSE

TASTE

SUPPLIED BY

CONTACT NAME/NUMBER

DATE OF PURCHASE

PRICE PAID – BOTTLE CASK

AGE WHEN BOTTLED

BOTTLED ABV %

DATE OF DISTILLATION

DATE OF BOTTLING

BOTTLE NUMBER CASK NUMBER

CASK TYPE CASK SIZE

COMMENTS

MALT

DISTILLERY

SPEYSIDE ☐ HIGHLAND NORTHERN ☐ HIGHLAND EASTERN ☐ HIGHLAND WESTERN ☐ HIGHLAND SOUTHERN ☐ LOWLAND ☐ ISLAY ☐ ISLANDS ☐ CAMPBELTOWN ☐ IRELAND ☐ OTHER ☐

APPEARANCE

FULL STRENGTH

NOSE

TASTE

FIRST REDUCTION

NOSE

TASTE

SUPPLIED BY

CONTACT NAME/NUMBER

DATE OF PURCHASE

PRICE PAID – BOTTLE CASK

AGE WHEN BOTTLED

BOTTLED ABV %

DATE OF DISTILLATION

DATE OF BOTTLING

BOTTLE NUMBER CASK NUMBER

CASK TYPE CASK SIZE

COMMENTS

MALT

DISTILLERY

SPEYSIDE ☐ HIGHLAND NORTHERN ☐ HIGHLAND EASTERN ☐ HIGHLAND WESTERN ☐ HIGHLAND SOUTHERN ☐ LOWLAND ☐ ISLAY ☐ ISLANDS ☐ CAMPBELTOWN ☐ IRELAND ☐ OTHER ☐

APPEARANCE

FULL STRENGTH

NOSE

TASTE

FIRST REDUCTION

NOSE

TASTE

SUPPLIED BY

CONTACT NAME/NUMBER

DATE OF PURCHASE

PRICE PAID – BOTTLE CASK

AGE WHEN BOTTLED

BOTTLED ABV %

DATE OF DISTILLATION

DATE OF BOTTLING

BOTTLE NUMBER CASK NUMBER

CASK TYPE CASK SIZE

COMMENTS

MALT DISTILLERY

SPEYSIDE ☐ HIGHLAND NORTHERN ☐ HIGHLAND EASTERN ☐ HIGHLAND WESTERN ☐ HIGHLAND SOUTHERN ☐ LOWLAND ☐ ISLAY ☐ ISLANDS ☐ CAMPBELTOWN ☐ IRELAND ☐ OTHER ☐

APPEARANCE

FULL STRENGTH

NOSE

TASTE

FIRST REDUCTION

NOSE

TASTE

SUPPLIED BY

CONTACT NAME/NUMBER

DATE OF PURCHASE

PRICE PAID – BOTTLE CASK

AGE WHEN BOTTLED

BOTTLED ABV %

DATE OF DISTILLATION

DATE OF BOTTLING

BOTTLE NUMBER CASK NUMBER

CASK TYPE CASK SIZE

COMMENTS

MALT

DISTILLERY

SPEYSIDE ☐ HIGHLAND NORTHERN ☐ HIGHLAND EASTERN ☐ HIGHLAND WESTERN ☐ HIGHLAND SOUTHERN ☐ LOWLAND ☐ ISLAY ☐ ISLANDS ☐ CAMPBELTOWN ☐ IRELAND ☐ OTHER ☐

APPEARANCE

FULL STRENGTH

NOSE

TASTE

FIRST REDUCTION

NOSE

TASTE

SUPPLIED BY

CONTACT NAME/NUMBER

DATE OF PURCHASE

PRICE PAID – BOTTLE　　CASK

AGE WHEN BOTTLED

BOTTLED ABV %

DATE OF DISTILLATION

DATE OF BOTTLING

BOTTLE NUMBER　　CASK NUMBER

CASK TYPE　　CASK SIZE

COMMENTS

MALT

DISTILLERY

SPEYSIDE ☐ HIGHLAND NORTHERN ☐ HIGHLAND EASTERN ☐ HIGHLAND WESTERN ☐ HIGHLAND SOUTHERN ☐ LOWLAND ☐ ISLAY ☐ ISLANDS ☐ CAMPBELTOWN ☐ IRELAND ☐ OTHER ☐

APPEARANCE

FULL STRENGTH

NOSE

TASTE

FIRST REDUCTION

NOSE

TASTE

SUPPLIED BY

CONTACT NAME/NUMBER

DATE OF PURCHASE

PRICE PAID – BOTTLE CASK

AGE WHEN BOTTLED

BOTTLED ABV %

DATE OF DISTILLATION

DATE OF BOTTLING

BOTTLE NUMBER CASK NUMBER

CASK TYPE CASK SIZE

COMMENTS

MALT

DISTILLERY

SPEYSIDE ☐ HIGHLAND NORTHERN ☐ HIGHLAND EASTERN ☐ HIGHLAND WESTERN ☐ HIGHLAND SOUTHERN ☐ LOWLAND ☐ ISLAY ☐ ISLANDS ☐ CAMPBELTOWN ☐ IRELAND ☐ OTHER ☐

APPEARANCE

FULL STRENGTH

NOSE

TASTE

FIRST REDUCTION

NOSE

TASTE

SUPPLIED BY

CONTACT NAME/NUMBER

DATE OF PURCHASE

PRICE PAID – BOTTLE CASK

AGE WHEN BOTTLED

BOTTLED ABV %

DATE OF DISTILLATION

DATE OF BOTTLING

BOTTLE NUMBER CASK NUMBER

CASK TYPE CASK SIZE

COMMENTS

MALT

DISTILLERY

SPEYSIDE ☐ HIGHLAND NORTHERN ☐ HIGHLAND EASTERN ☐ HIGHLAND WESTERN ☐ HIGHLAND SOUTHERN ☐ LOWLAND ☐ ISLAY ☐ ISLANDS ☐ CAMPBELTOWN ☐ IRELAND ☐ OTHER ☐

APPEARANCE

FULL STRENGTH

NOSE

TASTE

FIRST REDUCTION

NOSE

TASTE

SUPPLIED BY

CONTACT NAME/NUMBER

DATE OF PURCHASE

PRICE PAID – BOTTLE CASK

AGE WHEN BOTTLED

BOTTLED ABV %

DATE OF DISTILLATION

DATE OF BOTTLING

BOTTLE NUMBER CASK NUMBER

CASK TYPE CASK SIZE

COMMENTS

MALT

DISTILLERY

SPEYSIDE ☐ HIGHLAND NORTHERN ☐ HIGHLAND EASTERN ☐ HIGHLAND WESTERN ☐ HIGHLAND SOUTHERN ☐ LOWLAND ☐ ISLAY ☐ ISLANDS ☐ CAMPBELTOWN ☐ IRELAND ☐ OTHER ☐

APPEARANCE

FULL STRENGTH

NOSE

TASTE

FIRST REDUCTION

NOSE

TASTE

SUPPLIED BY

CONTACT NAME/NUMBER

DATE OF PURCHASE

PRICE PAID – BOTTLE CASK

AGE WHEN BOTTLED

BOTTLED ABV %

DATE OF DISTILLATION

DATE OF BOTTLING

BOTTLE NUMBER CASK NUMBER

CASK TYPE CASK SIZE

COMMENTS

MALT

DISTILLERY

SPEYSIDE ☐ HIGHLAND NORTHERN ☐ HIGHLAND EASTERN ☐ HIGHLAND WESTERN ☐ HIGHLAND SOUTHERN ☐ LOWLAND ☐ ISLAY ☐ ISLANDS ☐ CAMPBELTOWN ☐ IRELAND ☐ OTHER ☐

APPEARANCE

FULL STRENGTH

NOSE

TASTE

FIRST REDUCTION

NOSE

TASTE

SUPPLIED BY

CONTACT NAME/NUMBER

DATE OF PURCHASE

PRICE PAID – BOTTLE CASK

AGE WHEN BOTTLED

BOTTLED ABV %

DATE OF DISTILLATION

DATE OF BOTTLING

BOTTLE NUMBER CASK NUMBER

CASK TYPE CASK SIZE

COMMENTS

MALT

DISTILLERY

SPEYSIDE ☐ HIGHLAND NORTHERN ☐ HIGHLAND EASTERN ☐ HIGHLAND WESTERN ☐ HIGHLAND SOUTHERN ☐ LOWLAND ☐ ISLAY ☐ ISLANDS ☐ CAMPBELTOWN ☐ IRELAND ☐ OTHER ☐

APPEARANCE

FULL STRENGTH

NOSE

TASTE

FIRST REDUCTION

NOSE

TASTE

SUPPLIED BY

CONTACT NAME/NUMBER

DATE OF PURCHASE

PRICE PAID – BOTTLE CASK

AGE WHEN BOTTLED

BOTTLED ABV %

DATE OF DISTILLATION

DATE OF BOTTLING

BOTTLE NUMBER CASK NUMBER

CASK TYPE CASK SIZE

COMMENTS

MALT

DISTILLERY

SPEYSIDE ☐ HIGHLAND NORTHERN ☐ HIGHLAND EASTERN ☐ HIGHLAND WESTERN ☐ HIGHLAND SOUTHERN ☐ LOWLAND ☐ ISLAY ☐ ISLANDS ☐ CAMPBELTOWN ☐ IRELAND ☐ OTHER ☐

APPEARANCE

FULL STRENGTH

NOSE

TASTE

FIRST REDUCTION

NOSE

TASTE

SUPPLIED BY

CONTACT NAME/NUMBER

DATE OF PURCHASE

PRICE PAID – BOTTLE CASK

AGE WHEN BOTTLED

BOTTLED ABV %

DATE OF DISTILLATION

DATE OF BOTTLING

BOTTLE NUMBER CASK NUMBER

CASK TYPE CASK SIZE

COMMENTS

MALT

DISTILLERY

SPEYSIDE ☐ HIGHLAND NORTHERN ☐ HIGHLAND EASTERN ☐ HIGHLAND WESTERN ☐ HIGHLAND SOUTHERN ☐ LOWLAND ☐ ISLAY ☐ ISLANDS ☐ CAMPBELTOWN ☐ IRELAND ☐ OTHER ☐

APPEARANCE

FULL STRENGTH

NOSE

TASTE

FIRST REDUCTION

NOSE

TASTE

SUPPLIED BY

CONTACT NAME/NUMBER

DATE OF PURCHASE

PRICE PAID – BOTTLE CASK

AGE WHEN BOTTLED

BOTTLED ABV %

DATE OF DISTILLATION

DATE OF BOTTLING

BOTTLE NUMBER CASK NUMBER

CASK TYPE CASK SIZE

COMMENTS

MALT

DISTILLERY

SPEYSIDE ☐ HIGHLAND NORTHERN ☐ HIGHLAND EASTERN ☐ HIGHLAND WESTERN ☐ HIGHLAND SOUTHERN ☐ LOWLAND ☐ ISLAY ☐ ISLANDS ☐ CAMPBELTOWN ☐ IRELAND ☐ OTHER ☐

APPEARANCE

FULL STRENGTH

NOSE

TASTE

FIRST REDUCTION

NOSE

TASTE

SUPPLIED BY

CONTACT NAME/NUMBER

DATE OF PURCHASE

PRICE PAID – BOTTLE CASK

AGE WHEN BOTTLED

BOTTLED ABV %

DATE OF DISTILLATION

DATE OF BOTTLING

BOTTLE NUMBER CASK NUMBER

CASK TYPE CASK SIZE

COMMENTS

MALT

DISTILLERY

SPEYSIDE ☐ HIGHLAND NORTHERN ☐ HIGHLAND EASTERN ☐ HIGHLAND WESTERN ☐ HIGHLAND SOUTHERN ☐ LOWLAND ☐ ISLAY ☐ ISLANDS ☐ CAMPBELTOWN ☐ IRELAND ☐ OTHER ☐

APPEARANCE

FULL STRENGTH

NOSE

TASTE

FIRST REDUCTION

NOSE

TASTE

SUPPLIED BY

CONTACT NAME/NUMBER

DATE OF PURCHASE

PRICE PAID – BOTTLE CASK

AGE WHEN BOTTLED

BOTTLED ABV %

DATE OF DISTILLATION

DATE OF BOTTLING

BOTTLE NUMBER CASK NUMBER

CASK TYPE CASK SIZE

COMMENTS

MALT

DISTILLERY

SPEYSIDE ☐ HIGHLAND NORTHERN ☐ HIGHLAND EASTERN ☐ HIGHLAND WESTERN ☐ HIGHLAND SOUTHERN ☐ LOWLAND ☐ ISLAY ☐ ISLANDS ☐ CAMPBELTOWN ☐ IRELAND ☐ OTHER ☐

APPEARANCE

FULL STRENGTH

NOSE

TASTE

FIRST REDUCTION

NOSE

TASTE

SUPPLIED BY

CONTACT NAME/NUMBER

DATE OF PURCHASE

PRICE PAID – BOTTLE CASK

AGE WHEN BOTTLED

BOTTLED ABV %

DATE OF DISTILLATION

DATE OF BOTTLING

BOTTLE NUMBER CASK NUMBER

CASK TYPE CASK SIZE

COMMENTS

MALT

DISTILLERY

SPEYSIDE ☐ HIGHLAND NORTHERN ☐ HIGHLAND EASTERN ☐ HIGHLAND WESTERN ☐ HIGHLAND SOUTHERN ☐ LOWLAND ☐ ISLAY ☐ ISLANDS ☐ CAMPBELTOWN ☐ IRELAND ☐ OTHER ☐

APPEARANCE

FULL STRENGTH

NOSE

TASTE

FIRST REDUCTION

NOSE

TASTE

SUPPLIED BY

CONTACT NAME/NUMBER

DATE OF PURCHASE

PRICE PAID – BOTTLE CASK

AGE WHEN BOTTLED

BOTTLED ABV %

DATE OF DISTILLATION

DATE OF BOTTLING

BOTTLE NUMBER CASK NUMBER

CASK TYPE CASK SIZE

COMMENTS

MALT

DISTILLERY

SPEYSIDE ☐ HIGHLAND NORTHERN ☐ HIGHLAND EASTERN ☐ HIGHLAND WESTERN ☐ HIGHLAND SOUTHERN ☐ LOWLAND ☐ ISLAY ☐ ISLANDS ☐ CAMPBELTOWN ☐ IRELAND ☐ OTHER ☐

APPEARANCE

FULL STRENGTH

NOSE

TASTE

FIRST REDUCTION

NOSE

TASTE

SUPPLIED BY

CONTACT NAME/NUMBER

DATE OF PURCHASE

PRICE PAID – BOTTLE CASK

AGE WHEN BOTTLED

BOTTLED ABV %

DATE OF DISTILLATION

DATE OF BOTTLING

BOTTLE NUMBER CASK NUMBER

CASK TYPE CASK SIZE

COMMENTS

MALT

DISTILLERY

SPEYSIDE ☐ HIGHLAND NORTHERN ☐ HIGHLAND EASTERN ☐ HIGHLAND WESTERN ☐ HIGHLAND SOUTHERN ☐ LOWLAND ☐ ISLAY ☐ ISLANDS ☐ CAMPBELTOWN ☐ IRELAND ☐ OTHER ☐

APPEARANCE

FULL STRENGTH

NOSE

TASTE

FIRST REDUCTION

NOSE

TASTE

SUPPLIED BY

CONTACT NAME/NUMBER

DATE OF PURCHASE

PRICE PAID – BOTTLE CASK

AGE WHEN BOTTLED

BOTTLED ABV %

DATE OF DISTILLATION

DATE OF BOTTLING

BOTTLE NUMBER CASK NUMBER

CASK TYPE CASK SIZE

COMMENTS

MALT | DISTILLERY

SPEYSIDE ☐ HIGHLAND NORTHERN ☐ HIGHLAND EASTERN ☐ HIGHLAND WESTERN ☐ HIGHLAND SOUTHERN ☐ LOWLAND ☐ ISLAY ☐ ISLANDS ☐ CAMPBELTOWN ☐ IRELAND ☐ OTHER ☐

APPEARANCE

FULL STRENGTH

NOSE

TASTE

FIRST REDUCTION

NOSE

TASTE

SUPPLIED BY

CONTACT NAME/NUMBER

DATE OF PURCHASE

PRICE PAID – BOTTLE | CASK

AGE WHEN BOTTLED

BOTTLED ABV %

DATE OF DISTILLATION

DATE OF BOTTLING

BOTTLE NUMBER | CASK NUMBER

CASK TYPE | CASK SIZE

COMMENTS

MALT

DISTILLERY

SPEYSIDE ☐ HIGHLAND NORTHERN ☐ HIGHLAND EASTERN ☐ HIGHLAND WESTERN ☐ HIGHLAND SOUTHERN ☐ LOWLAND ☐ ISLAY ☐ ISLANDS ☐ CAMPBELTOWN ☐ IRELAND ☐ OTHER ☐

APPEARANCE

FULL STRENGTH

NOSE

TASTE

FIRST REDUCTION

NOSE

TASTE

SUPPLIED BY

CONTACT NAME/NUMBER

DATE OF PURCHASE

PRICE PAID – BOTTLE CASK

AGE WHEN BOTTLED

BOTTLED ABV %

DATE OF DISTILLATION

DATE OF BOTTLING

BOTTLE NUMBER CASK NUMBER

CASK TYPE CASK SIZE

COMMENTS

MALT

DISTILLERY

SPEYSIDE ☐ HIGHLAND NORTHERN ☐ HIGHLAND EASTERN ☐ HIGHLAND WESTERN ☐ HIGHLAND SOUTHERN ☐ LOWLAND ☐ ISLAY ☐ ISLANDS ☐ CAMPBELTOWN ☐ IRELAND ☐ OTHER ☐

APPEARANCE

FULL STRENGTH

NOSE

TASTE

FIRST REDUCTION

NOSE

TASTE

SUPPLIED BY

CONTACT NAME/NUMBER

DATE OF PURCHASE

PRICE PAID – BOTTLE CASK

AGE WHEN BOTTLED

BOTTLED ABV %

DATE OF DISTILLATION

DATE OF BOTTLING

BOTTLE NUMBER CASK NUMBER

CASK TYPE CASK SIZE

COMMENTS

MALT

DISTILLERY

SPEYSIDE ☐ HIGHLAND NORTHERN ☐ HIGHLAND EASTERN ☐ HIGHLAND WESTERN ☐ HIGHLAND SOUTHERN ☐ LOWLAND ☐ ISLAY ☐ ISLANDS ☐ CAMPBELTOWN ☐ IRELAND ☐ OTHER ☐

APPEARANCE

FULL STRENGTH

NOSE

TASTE

FIRST REDUCTION

NOSE

TASTE

SUPPLIED BY

CONTACT NAME/NUMBER

DATE OF PURCHASE

PRICE PAID – BOTTLE CASK

AGE WHEN BOTTLED

BOTTLED ABV %

DATE OF DISTILLATION

DATE OF BOTTLING

BOTTLE NUMBER CASK NUMBER

CASK TYPE CASK SIZE

COMMENTS

MALT

DISTILLERY

SPEYSIDE ☐ HIGHLAND NORTHERN ☐ HIGHLAND EASTERN ☐ HIGHLAND WESTERN ☐ HIGHLAND SOUTHERN ☐ LOWLAND ☐ ISLAY ☐ ISLANDS ☐ CAMPBELTOWN ☐ IRELAND ☐ OTHER ☐

APPEARANCE

FULL STRENGTH

NOSE

TASTE

FIRST REDUCTION

NOSE

TASTE

SUPPLIED BY

CONTACT NAME/NUMBER

DATE OF PURCHASE

PRICE PAID – BOTTLE CASK

AGE WHEN BOTTLED

BOTTLED ABV %

DATE OF DISTILLATION

DATE OF BOTTLING

BOTTLE NUMBER CASK NUMBER

CASK TYPE CASK SIZE

COMMENTS

MALT

DISTILLERY

SPEYSIDE ☐ HIGHLAND NORTHERN ☐ HIGHLAND EASTERN ☐ HIGHLAND WESTERN ☐ HIGHLAND SOUTHERN ☐ LOWLAND ☐ ISLAY ☐ ISLANDS ☐ CAMPBELTOWN ☐ IRELAND ☐ OTHER ☐

APPEARANCE

FULL STRENGTH

NOSE

TASTE

FIRST REDUCTION

NOSE

TASTE

SUPPLIED BY

CONTACT NAME/NUMBER

DATE OF PURCHASE

PRICE PAID – BOTTLE CASK

AGE WHEN BOTTLED

BOTTLED ABV %

DATE OF DISTILLATION

DATE OF BOTTLING

BOTTLE NUMBER CASK NUMBER

CASK TYPE CASK SIZE

COMMENTS

MALT

DISTILLERY

SPEYSIDE ☐ HIGHLAND NORTHERN ☐ HIGHLAND EASTERN ☐ HIGHLAND WESTERN ☐ HIGHLAND SOUTHERN ☐ LOWLAND ☐ ISLAY ☐ ISLANDS ☐ CAMPBELTOWN ☐ IRELAND ☐ OTHER ☐

APPEARANCE

FULL STRENGTH

NOSE

TASTE

FIRST REDUCTION

NOSE

TASTE

SUPPLIED BY

CONTACT NAME/NUMBER

DATE OF PURCHASE

PRICE PAID – BOTTLE CASK

AGE WHEN BOTTLED

BOTTLED ABV %

DATE OF DISTILLATION

DATE OF BOTTLING

BOTTLE NUMBER CASK NUMBER

CASK TYPE CASK SIZE

COMMENTS

MALT

DISTILLERY

SPEYSIDE ☐ HIGHLAND NORTHERN ☐ HIGHLAND EASTERN ☐ HIGHLAND WESTERN ☐ HIGHLAND SOUTHERN ☐ LOWLAND ☐ ISLAY ☐ ISLANDS ☐ CAMPBELTOWN ☐ IRELAND ☐ OTHER ☐

APPEARANCE

FULL STRENGTH

NOSE

TASTE

FIRST REDUCTION

NOSE

TASTE

SUPPLIED BY

CONTACT NAME/NUMBER

DATE OF PURCHASE

PRICE PAID – BOTTLE CASK

AGE WHEN BOTTLED

BOTTLED ABV %

DATE OF DISTILLATION

DATE OF BOTTLING

BOTTLE NUMBER CASK NUMBER

CASK TYPE CASK SIZE

COMMENTS

MALT

DISTILLERY

SPEYSIDE ☐ HIGHLAND NORTHERN ☐ HIGHLAND EASTERN ☐ HIGHLAND WESTERN ☐ HIGHLAND SOUTHERN ☐ LOWLAND ☐ ISLAY ☐ ISLANDS ☐ CAMPBELTOWN ☐ IRELAND ☐ OTHER ☐

APPEARANCE

FULL STRENGTH

NOSE

TASTE

FIRST REDUCTION

NOSE

TASTE

SUPPLIED BY

CONTACT NAME/NUMBER

DATE OF PURCHASE

PRICE PAID – BOTTLE CASK

AGE WHEN BOTTLED

BOTTLED ABV %

DATE OF DISTILLATION

DATE OF BOTTLING

BOTTLE NUMBER CASK NUMBER

CASK TYPE CASK SIZE

COMMENTS

MALT

DISTILLERY

SPEYSIDE ☐ HIGHLAND NORTHERN ☐ HIGHLAND EASTERN ☐ HIGHLAND WESTERN ☐ HIGHLAND SOUTHERN ☐ LOWLAND ☐ ISLAY ☐ ISLANDS ☐ CAMPBELTOWN ☐ IRELAND ☐ OTHER ☐

APPEARANCE

FULL STRENGTH

NOSE

TASTE

FIRST REDUCTION

NOSE

TASTE

SUPPLIED BY

CONTACT NAME/NUMBER

DATE OF PURCHASE

PRICE PAID – BOTTLE CASK

AGE WHEN BOTTLED

BOTTLED ABV %

DATE OF DISTILLATION

DATE OF BOTTLING

BOTTLE NUMBER CASK NUMBER

CASK TYPE CASK SIZE

COMMENTS

MALT

DISTILLERY

SPEYSIDE ☐ HIGHLAND NORTHERN ☐ HIGHLAND EASTERN ☐ HIGHLAND WESTERN ☐ HIGHLAND SOUTHERN ☐ LOWLAND ☐ ISLAY ☐ ISLANDS ☐ CAMPBELTOWN ☐ IRELAND ☐ OTHER ☐

APPEARANCE

FULL STRENGTH

NOSE

TASTE

FIRST REDUCTION

NOSE

TASTE

SUPPLIED BY

CONTACT NAME/NUMBER

DATE OF PURCHASE

PRICE PAID – BOTTLE CASK

AGE WHEN BOTTLED

BOTTLED ABV %

DATE OF DISTILLATION

DATE OF BOTTLING

BOTTLE NUMBER CASK NUMBER

CASK TYPE CASK SIZE

COMMENTS

MALT

DISTILLERY

SPEYSIDE ☐ HIGHLAND NORTHERN ☐ HIGHLAND EASTERN ☐ HIGHLAND WESTERN ☐ HIGHLAND SOUTHERN ☐ LOWLAND ☐ ISLAY ☐ ISLANDS ☐ CAMPBELTOWN ☐ IRELAND ☐ OTHER ☐

APPEARANCE

FULL STRENGTH

NOSE

TASTE

FIRST REDUCTION

NOSE

TASTE

SUPPLIED BY

CONTACT NAME/NUMBER

DATE OF PURCHASE

PRICE PAID – BOTTLE CASK

AGE WHEN BOTTLED

BOTTLED ABV %

DATE OF DISTILLATION

DATE OF BOTTLING

BOTTLE NUMBER CASK NUMBER

CASK TYPE CASK SIZE

COMMENTS

MALT

DISTILLERY

SPEYSIDE ☐ HIGHLAND NORTHERN ☐ HIGHLAND EASTERN ☐ HIGHLAND WESTERN ☐ HIGHLAND SOUTHERN ☐ LOWLAND ☐ ISLAY ☐ ISLANDS ☐ CAMPBELTOWN ☐ IRELAND ☐ OTHER ☐

APPEARANCE

FULL STRENGTH

NOSE

TASTE

FIRST REDUCTION

NOSE

TASTE

SUPPLIED BY

CONTACT NAME/NUMBER

DATE OF PURCHASE

PRICE PAID – BOTTLE CASK

AGE WHEN BOTTLED

BOTTLED ABV %

DATE OF DISTILLATION

DATE OF BOTTLING

BOTTLE NUMBER CASK NUMBER

CASK TYPE CASK SIZE

COMMENTS

MALT

DISTILLERY

SPEYSIDE ☐ HIGHLAND NORTHERN ☐ HIGHLAND EASTERN ☐ HIGHLAND WESTERN ☐ HIGHLAND SOUTHERN ☐ LOWLAND ☐ ISLAY ☐ ISLANDS ☐ CAMPBELTOWN ☐ IRELAND ☐ OTHER ☐

APPEARANCE

FULL STRENGTH

NOSE

TASTE

FIRST REDUCTION

NOSE

TASTE

SUPPLIED BY

CONTACT NAME/NUMBER

DATE OF PURCHASE

PRICE PAID – BOTTLE CASK

AGE WHEN BOTTLED

BOTTLED ABV %

DATE OF DISTILLATION

DATE OF BOTTLING

BOTTLE NUMBER CASK NUMBER

CASK TYPE CASK SIZE

COMMENTS

MALT

DISTILLERY

SPEYSIDE ☐ HIGHLAND NORTHERN ☐ HIGHLAND EASTERN ☐ HIGHLAND WESTERN ☐ HIGHLAND SOUTHERN ☐ LOWLAND ☐ ISLAY ☐ ISLANDS ☐ CAMPBELTOWN ☐ IRELAND ☐ OTHER ☐

APPEARANCE

FULL STRENGTH

NOSE

TASTE

FIRST REDUCTION

NOSE

TASTE

SUPPLIED BY

CONTACT NAME/NUMBER

DATE OF PURCHASE

PRICE PAID – BOTTLE CASK

AGE WHEN BOTTLED

BOTTLED ABV %

DATE OF DISTILLATION

DATE OF BOTTLING

BOTTLE NUMBER CASK NUMBER

CASK TYPE CASK SIZE

COMMENTS

MALT

DISTILLERY

SPEYSIDE ☐ HIGHLAND NORTHERN ☐ HIGHLAND EASTERN ☐ HIGHLAND WESTERN ☐ HIGHLAND SOUTHERN ☐ LOWLAND ☐ ISLAY ☐ ISLANDS ☐ CAMPBELTOWN ☐ IRELAND ☐ OTHER ☐

APPEARANCE

FULL STRENGTH

NOSE

TASTE

FIRST REDUCTION

NOSE

TASTE

SUPPLIED BY

CONTACT NAME/NUMBER

DATE OF PURCHASE

PRICE PAID – BOTTLE CASK

AGE WHEN BOTTLED

BOTTLED ABV %

DATE OF DISTILLATION

DATE OF BOTTLING

BOTTLE NUMBER CASK NUMBER

CASK TYPE CASK SIZE

COMMENTS

MALT

DISTILLERY

SPEYSIDE ☐ HIGHLAND NORTHERN ☐ HIGHLAND EASTERN ☐ HIGHLAND WESTERN ☐ HIGHLAND SOUTHERN ☐ LOWLAND ☐ ISLAY ☐ ISLANDS ☐ CAMPBELTOWN ☐ IRELAND ☐ OTHER ☐

APPEARANCE

FULL STRENGTH

NOSE

TASTE

FIRST REDUCTION

NOSE

TASTE

SUPPLIED BY

CONTACT NAME/NUMBER

DATE OF PURCHASE

PRICE PAID – BOTTLE CASK

AGE WHEN BOTTLED

BOTTLED ABV %

DATE OF DISTILLATION

DATE OF BOTTLING

BOTTLE NUMBER CASK NUMBER

CASK TYPE CASK SIZE

COMMENTS

MALT

DISTILLERY

SPEYSIDE ☐ HIGHLAND NORTHERN ☐ HIGHLAND EASTERN ☐ HIGHLAND WESTERN ☐ HIGHLAND SOUTHERN ☐ LOWLAND ☐ ISLAY ☐ ISLANDS ☐ CAMPBELTOWN ☐ IRELAND ☐ OTHER ☐

APPEARANCE

FULL STRENGTH

NOSE

TASTE

FIRST REDUCTION

NOSE

TASTE

SUPPLIED BY

CONTACT NAME/NUMBER

DATE OF PURCHASE

PRICE PAID – BOTTLE CASK

AGE WHEN BOTTLED

BOTTLED ABV %

DATE OF DISTILLATION

DATE OF BOTTLING

BOTTLE NUMBER CASK NUMBER

CASK TYPE CASK SIZE

COMMENTS

MALT

DISTILLERY

SPEYSIDE ☐ HIGHLAND NORTHERN ☐ HIGHLAND EASTERN ☐ HIGHLAND WESTERN ☐ HIGHLAND SOUTHERN ☐ LOWLAND ☐ ISLAY ☐ ISLANDS ☐ CAMPBELTOWN ☐ IRELAND ☐ OTHER ☐

APPEARANCE

FULL STRENGTH

NOSE

TASTE

FIRST REDUCTION

NOSE

TASTE

SUPPLIED BY

CONTACT NAME/NUMBER

DATE OF PURCHASE

PRICE PAID – BOTTLE CASK

AGE WHEN BOTTLED

BOTTLED ABV %

DATE OF DISTILLATION

DATE OF BOTTLING

BOTTLE NUMBER CASK NUMBER

CASK TYPE CASK SIZE

COMMENTS

MALT

DISTILLERY

SPEYSIDE ☐ HIGHLAND NORTHERN ☐ HIGHLAND EASTERN ☐ HIGHLAND WESTERN ☐ HIGHLAND SOUTHERN ☐ LOWLAND ☐ ISLAY ☐ ISLANDS ☐ CAMPBELTOWN ☐ IRELAND ☐ OTHER ☐

APPEARANCE

FULL STRENGTH

NOSE

TASTE

FIRST REDUCTION

NOSE

TASTE

SUPPLIED BY

CONTACT NAME/NUMBER

DATE OF PURCHASE

PRICE PAID – BOTTLE CASK

AGE WHEN BOTTLED

BOTTLED ABV %

DATE OF DISTILLATION

DATE OF BOTTLING

BOTTLE NUMBER CASK NUMBER

CASK TYPE CASK SIZE

COMMENTS

MALT

DISTILLERY

SPEYSIDE ☐ HIGHLAND NORTHERN ☐ HIGHLAND EASTERN ☐ HIGHLAND WESTERN ☐ HIGHLAND SOUTHERN ☐ LOWLAND ☐ ISLAY ☐ ISLANDS ☐ CAMPBELTOWN ☐ IRELAND ☐ OTHER ☐

APPEARANCE

FULL STRENGTH

NOSE

TASTE

FIRST REDUCTION

NOSE

TASTE

SUPPLIED BY

CONTACT NAME/NUMBER

DATE OF PURCHASE

PRICE PAID – BOTTLE CASK

AGE WHEN BOTTLED

BOTTLED ABV %

DATE OF DISTILLATION

DATE OF BOTTLING

BOTTLE NUMBER CASK NUMBER

CASK TYPE CASK SIZE

COMMENTS

MALT

DISTILLERY

SPEYSIDE ☐ HIGHLAND NORTHERN ☐ HIGHLAND EASTERN ☐ HIGHLAND WESTERN ☐ HIGHLAND SOUTHERN ☐ LOWLAND ☐ ISLAY ☐ ISLANDS ☐ CAMPBELTOWN ☐ IRELAND ☐ OTHER ☐

APPEARANCE

FULL STRENGTH

NOSE

TASTE

FIRST REDUCTION

NOSE

TASTE

SUPPLIED BY

CONTACT NAME/NUMBER

DATE OF PURCHASE

PRICE PAID – BOTTLE CASK

AGE WHEN BOTTLED

BOTTLED ABV %

DATE OF DISTILLATION

DATE OF BOTTLING

BOTTLE NUMBER CASK NUMBER

CASK TYPE CASK SIZE

COMMENTS

MALT

DISTILLERY

SPEYSIDE ☐ HIGHLAND NORTHERN ☐ HIGHLAND EASTERN ☐ HIGHLAND WESTERN ☐ HIGHLAND SOUTHERN ☐ LOWLAND ☐ ISLAY ☐ ISLANDS ☐ CAMPBELTOWN ☐ IRELAND ☐ OTHER ☐

APPEARANCE

FULL STRENGTH

NOSE

TASTE

FIRST REDUCTION

NOSE

TASTE

SUPPLIED BY

CONTACT NAME/NUMBER

DATE OF PURCHASE

PRICE PAID – BOTTLE CASK

AGE WHEN BOTTLED

BOTTLED ABV %

DATE OF DISTILLATION

DATE OF BOTTLING

BOTTLE NUMBER CASK NUMBER

CASK TYPE CASK SIZE

COMMENTS

MALT

DISTILLERY

SPEYSIDE ☐ HIGHLAND NORTHERN ☐ HIGHLAND EASTERN ☐ HIGHLAND WESTERN ☐ HIGHLAND SOUTHERN ☐ LOWLAND ☐ ISLAY ☐ ISLANDS ☐ CAMPBELTOWN ☐ IRELAND ☐ OTHER ☐

APPEARANCE

FULL STRENGTH

NOSE

TASTE

FIRST REDUCTION

NOSE

TASTE

SUPPLIED BY

CONTACT NAME/NUMBER

DATE OF PURCHASE

PRICE PAID – BOTTLE CASK

AGE WHEN BOTTLED

BOTTLED ABV %

DATE OF DISTILLATION

DATE OF BOTTLING

BOTTLE NUMBER CASK NUMBER

CASK TYPE CASK SIZE

COMMENTS

MALT

DISTILLERY

SPEYSIDE ☐ HIGHLAND NORTHERN ☐ HIGHLAND EASTERN ☐ HIGHLAND WESTERN ☐ HIGHLAND SOUTHERN ☐ LOWLAND ☐ ISLAY ☐ ISLANDS ☐ CAMPBELTOWN ☐ IRELAND ☐ OTHER ☐

APPEARANCE

FULL STRENGTH

NOSE

TASTE

FIRST REDUCTION

NOSE

TASTE

SUPPLIED BY

CONTACT NAME/NUMBER

DATE OF PURCHASE

PRICE PAID – BOTTLE CASK

AGE WHEN BOTTLED

BOTTLED ABV %

DATE OF DISTILLATION

DATE OF BOTTLING

BOTTLE NUMBER CASK NUMBER

CASK TYPE CASK SIZE

COMMENTS

MALT DISTILLERY

SPEYSIDE ☐ HIGHLAND NORTHERN ☐ HIGHLAND EASTERN ☐ HIGHLAND WESTERN ☐ HIGHLAND SOUTHERN ☐ LOWLAND ☐ ISLAY ☐ ISLANDS ☐ CAMPBELTOWN ☐ IRELAND ☐ OTHER ☐

APPEARANCE

FULL STRENGTH

NOSE

TASTE

FIRST REDUCTION

NOSE

TASTE

SUPPLIED BY

CONTACT NAME/NUMBER

DATE OF PURCHASE

PRICE PAID – BOTTLE CASK

AGE WHEN BOTTLED

BOTTLED ABV %

DATE OF DISTILLATION

DATE OF BOTTLING

BOTTLE NUMBER CASK NUMBER

CASK TYPE CASK SIZE

COMMENTS

MALT

DISTILLERY

SPEYSIDE ☐ HIGHLAND NORTHERN ☐ HIGHLAND EASTERN ☐ HIGHLAND WESTERN ☐ HIGHLAND SOUTHERN ☐ LOWLAND ☐ ISLAY ☐ ISLANDS ☐ CAMPBELTOWN ☐ IRELAND ☐ OTHER ☐

APPEARANCE

FULL STRENGTH

NOSE

TASTE

FIRST REDUCTION

NOSE

TASTE

SUPPLIED BY

CONTACT NAME/NUMBER

DATE OF PURCHASE

PRICE PAID – BOTTLE CASK

AGE WHEN BOTTLED

BOTTLED ABV %

DATE OF DISTILLATION

DATE OF BOTTLING

BOTTLE NUMBER CASK NUMBER

CASK TYPE CASK SIZE

COMMENTS

MALT

DISTILLERY

SPEYSIDE ☐ HIGHLAND NORTHERN ☐ HIGHLAND EASTERN ☐ HIGHLAND WESTERN ☐ HIGHLAND SOUTHERN ☐ LOWLAND ☐ ISLAY ☐ ISLANDS ☐ CAMPBELTOWN ☐ IRELAND ☐ OTHER ☐

APPEARANCE

FULL STRENGTH

NOSE

TASTE

FIRST REDUCTION

NOSE

TASTE

SUPPLIED BY

CONTACT NAME/NUMBER

DATE OF PURCHASE

PRICE PAID – BOTTLE CASK

AGE WHEN BOTTLED

BOTTLED ABV %

DATE OF DISTILLATION

DATE OF BOTTLING

BOTTLE NUMBER CASK NUMBER

CASK TYPE CASK SIZE

COMMENTS

MALT

DISTILLERY

SPEYSIDE ☐ HIGHLAND NORTHERN ☐ HIGHLAND EASTERN ☐ HIGHLAND WESTERN ☐ HIGHLAND SOUTHERN ☐ LOWLAND ☐ ISLAY ☐ ISLANDS ☐ CAMPBELTOWN ☐ IRELAND ☐ OTHER ☐

APPEARANCE

FULL STRENGTH

NOSE

TASTE

FIRST REDUCTION

NOSE

TASTE

SUPPLIED BY

CONTACT NAME/NUMBER

DATE OF PURCHASE

PRICE PAID – BOTTLE CASK

AGE WHEN BOTTLED

BOTTLED ABV %

DATE OF DISTILLATION

DATE OF BOTTLING

BOTTLE NUMBER CASK NUMBER

CASK TYPE CASK SIZE

COMMENTS

MALT

DISTILLERY

SPEYSIDE ☐ HIGHLAND NORTHERN ☐ HIGHLAND EASTERN ☐ HIGHLAND WESTERN ☐ HIGHLAND SOUTHERN ☐ LOWLAND ☐ ISLAY ☐ ISLANDS ☐ CAMPBELTOWN ☐ IRELAND ☐ OTHER ☐

APPEARANCE

FULL STRENGTH

NOSE

TASTE

FIRST REDUCTION

NOSE

TASTE

SUPPLIED BY

CONTACT NAME/NUMBER

DATE OF PURCHASE

PRICE PAID – BOTTLE CASK

AGE WHEN BOTTLED

BOTTLED ABV %

DATE OF DISTILLATION

DATE OF BOTTLING

BOTTLE NUMBER CASK NUMBER

CASK TYPE CASK SIZE

COMMENTS

MALT

DISTILLERY

SPEYSIDE ☐ HIGHLAND NORTHERN ☐ HIGHLAND EASTERN ☐ HIGHLAND WESTERN ☐ HIGHLAND SOUTHERN ☐ LOWLAND ☐ ISLAY ☐ ISLANDS ☐ CAMPBELTOWN ☐ IRELAND ☐ OTHER ☐

APPEARANCE

FULL STRENGTH

NOSE

TASTE

FIRST REDUCTION

NOSE

TASTE

SUPPLIED BY

CONTACT NAME/NUMBER

DATE OF PURCHASE

PRICE PAID – BOTTLE CASK

AGE WHEN BOTTLED

BOTTLED ABV %

DATE OF DISTILLATION

DATE OF BOTTLING

BOTTLE NUMBER CASK NUMBER

CASK TYPE CASK SIZE

COMMENTS

MALT

DISTILLERY

SPEYSIDE ☐ HIGHLAND NORTHERN ☐ HIGHLAND EASTERN ☐ HIGHLAND WESTERN ☐ HIGHLAND SOUTHERN ☐ LOWLAND ☐ ISLAY ☐ ISLANDS ☐ CAMPBELTOWN ☐ IRELAND ☐ OTHER ☐

APPEARANCE

FULL STRENGTH

NOSE

TASTE

FIRST REDUCTION

NOSE

TASTE

SUPPLIED BY

CONTACT NAME/NUMBER

DATE OF PURCHASE

PRICE PAID – BOTTLE CASK

AGE WHEN BOTTLED

BOTTLED ABV %

DATE OF DISTILLATION

DATE OF BOTTLING

BOTTLE NUMBER CASK NUMBER

CASK TYPE CASK SIZE

COMMENTS

MALT

DISTILLERY

SPEYSIDE ☐ HIGHLAND NORTHERN ☐ HIGHLAND EASTERN ☐ HIGHLAND WESTERN ☐ HIGHLAND SOUTHERN ☐ LOWLAND ☐ ISLAY ☐ ISLANDS ☐ CAMPBELTOWN ☐ IRELAND ☐ OTHER ☐

APPEARANCE

FULL STRENGTH

NOSE

TASTE

FIRST REDUCTION

NOSE

TASTE

SUPPLIED BY

CONTACT NAME/NUMBER

DATE OF PURCHASE

PRICE PAID – BOTTLE CASK

AGE WHEN BOTTLED

BOTTLED ABV %

DATE OF DISTILLATION

DATE OF BOTTLING

BOTTLE NUMBER CASK NUMBER

CASK TYPE CASK SIZE

COMMENTS

MALT

DISTILLERY

SPEYSIDE ☐ HIGHLAND NORTHERN ☐ HIGHLAND EASTERN ☐ HIGHLAND WESTERN ☐ HIGHLAND SOUTHERN ☐ LOWLAND ☐ ISLAY ☐ ISLANDS ☐ CAMPBELTOWN ☐ IRELAND ☐ OTHER ☐

APPEARANCE

FULL STRENGTH

NOSE

TASTE

FIRST REDUCTION

NOSE

TASTE

SUPPLIED BY

CONTACT NAME/NUMBER

DATE OF PURCHASE

PRICE PAID – BOTTLE CASK

AGE WHEN BOTTLED

BOTTLED ABV %

DATE OF DISTILLATION

DATE OF BOTTLING

BOTTLE NUMBER CASK NUMBER

CASK TYPE CASK SIZE

COMMENTS

MALT | DISTILLERY

SPEYSIDE ☐ HIGHLAND NORTHERN ☐ HIGHLAND EASTERN ☐ HIGHLAND WESTERN ☐ HIGHLAND SOUTHERN ☐ LOWLAND ☐ ISLAY ☐ ISLANDS ☐ CAMPBELTOWN ☐ IRELAND ☐ OTHER ☐

APPEARANCE

FULL STRENGTH

NOSE

TASTE

FIRST REDUCTION

NOSE

TASTE

SUPPLIED BY

CONTACT NAME/NUMBER

DATE OF PURCHASE

PRICE PAID – BOTTLE | CASK

AGE WHEN BOTTLED

BOTTLED ABV %

DATE OF DISTILLATION

DATE OF BOTTLING

BOTTLE NUMBER | CASK NUMBER

CASK TYPE | CASK SIZE

COMMENTS

MALT

DISTILLERY

SPEYSIDE ☐ HIGHLAND NORTHERN ☐ HIGHLAND EASTERN ☐ HIGHLAND WESTERN ☐ HIGHLAND SOUTHERN ☐ LOWLAND ☐ ISLAY ☐ ISLANDS ☐ CAMPBELTOWN ☐ IRELAND ☐ OTHER ☐

APPEARANCE

FULL STRENGTH

NOSE

TASTE

FIRST REDUCTION

NOSE

TASTE

SUPPLIED BY

CONTACT NAME/NUMBER

DATE OF PURCHASE

PRICE PAID – BOTTLE CASK

AGE WHEN BOTTLED

BOTTLED ABV %

DATE OF DISTILLATION

DATE OF BOTTLING

BOTTLE NUMBER CASK NUMBER

CASK TYPE CASK SIZE

COMMENTS

MALT

DISTILLERY

SPEYSIDE ☐ HIGHLAND NORTHERN ☐ HIGHLAND EASTERN ☐ HIGHLAND WESTERN ☐ HIGHLAND SOUTHERN ☐ LOWLAND ☐ ISLAY ☐ ISLANDS ☐ CAMPBELTOWN ☐ IRELAND ☐ OTHER ☐

APPEARANCE

FULL STRENGTH

NOSE

TASTE

FIRST REDUCTION

NOSE

TASTE

SUPPLIED BY

CONTACT NAME/NUMBER

DATE OF PURCHASE

PRICE PAID – BOTTLE CASK

AGE WHEN BOTTLED

BOTTLED ABV %

DATE OF DISTILLATION

DATE OF BOTTLING

BOTTLE NUMBER CASK NUMBER

CASK TYPE CASK SIZE

COMMENTS

MALT

DISTILLERY

SPEYSIDE ☐ HIGHLAND NORTHERN ☐ HIGHLAND EASTERN ☐ HIGHLAND WESTERN ☐ HIGHLAND SOUTHERN ☐ LOWLAND ☐ ISLAY ☐ ISLANDS ☐ CAMPBELTOWN ☐ IRELAND ☐ OTHER ☐

APPEARANCE

FULL STRENGTH

NOSE

TASTE

FIRST REDUCTION

NOSE

TASTE

SUPPLIED BY

CONTACT NAME/NUMBER

DATE OF PURCHASE

PRICE PAID – BOTTLE CASK

AGE WHEN BOTTLED

BOTTLED ABV %

DATE OF DISTILLATION

DATE OF BOTTLING

BOTTLE NUMBER CASK NUMBER

CASK TYPE CASK SIZE

COMMENTS

MALT DISTILLERY

SPEYSIDE ☐ HIGHLAND NORTHERN ☐ HIGHLAND EASTERN ☐ HIGHLAND WESTERN ☐ HIGHLAND SOUTHERN ☐ LOWLAND ☐ ISLAY ☐ ISLANDS ☐ CAMPBELTOWN ☐ IRELAND ☐ OTHER ☐

APPEARANCE

FULL STRENGTH

NOSE

TASTE

FIRST REDUCTION

NOSE

TASTE

SUPPLIED BY

CONTACT NAME/NUMBER

DATE OF PURCHASE

PRICE PAID – BOTTLE CASK

AGE WHEN BOTTLED

BOTTLED ABV %

DATE OF DISTILLATION

DATE OF BOTTLING

BOTTLE NUMBER CASK NUMBER

CASK TYPE CASK SIZE

COMMENTS

MALT

DISTILLERY

SPEYSIDE ☐ HIGHLAND NORTHERN ☐ HIGHLAND EASTERN ☐ HIGHLAND WESTERN ☐ HIGHLAND SOUTHERN ☐ LOWLAND ☐ ISLAY ☐ ISLANDS ☐ CAMPBELTOWN ☐ IRELAND ☐ OTHER ☐

APPEARANCE

FULL STRENGTH

NOSE

TASTE

FIRST REDUCTION

NOSE

TASTE

SUPPLIED BY

CONTACT NAME/NUMBER

DATE OF PURCHASE

PRICE PAID – BOTTLE CASK

AGE WHEN BOTTLED

BOTTLED ABV %

DATE OF DISTILLATION

DATE OF BOTTLING

BOTTLE NUMBER CASK NUMBER

CASK TYPE CASK SIZE

COMMENTS

MALT

DISTILLERY

SPEYSIDE ☐ HIGHLAND NORTHERN ☐ HIGHLAND EASTERN ☐ HIGHLAND WESTERN ☐ HIGHLAND SOUTHERN ☐ LOWLAND ☐ ISLAY ☐ ISLANDS ☐ CAMPBELTOWN ☐ IRELAND ☐ OTHER ☐

APPEARANCE

FULL STRENGTH

NOSE

TASTE

FIRST REDUCTION

NOSE

TASTE

SUPPLIED BY

CONTACT NAME/NUMBER

DATE OF PURCHASE

PRICE PAID – BOTTLE CASK

AGE WHEN BOTTLED

BOTTLED ABV %

DATE OF DISTILLATION

DATE OF BOTTLING

BOTTLE NUMBER CASK NUMBER

CASK TYPE CASK SIZE

COMMENTS

MALT

DISTILLERY

SPEYSIDE ☐ HIGHLAND NORTHERN ☐ HIGHLAND EASTERN ☐ HIGHLAND WESTERN ☐ HIGHLAND SOUTHERN ☐ LOWLAND ☐ ISLAY ☐ ISLANDS ☐ CAMPBELTOWN ☐ IRELAND ☐ OTHER ☐

APPEARANCE

FULL STRENGTH

NOSE

TASTE

FIRST REDUCTION

NOSE

TASTE

SUPPLIED BY

CONTACT NAME/NUMBER

DATE OF PURCHASE

PRICE PAID – BOTTLE CASK

AGE WHEN BOTTLED

BOTTLED ABV %

DATE OF DISTILLATION

DATE OF BOTTLING

BOTTLE NUMBER CASK NUMBER

CASK TYPE CASK SIZE

COMMENTS

MALT

DISTILLERY

SPEYSIDE ☐ HIGHLAND NORTHERN ☐ HIGHLAND EASTERN ☐ HIGHLAND WESTERN ☐ HIGHLAND SOUTHERN ☐ LOWLAND ☐ ISLAY ☐ ISLANDS ☐ CAMPBELTOWN ☐ IRELAND ☐ OTHER ☐

APPEARANCE

FULL STRENGTH

NOSE

TASTE

FIRST REDUCTION

NOSE

TASTE

SUPPLIED BY

CONTACT NAME/NUMBER

DATE OF PURCHASE

PRICE PAID – BOTTLE CASK

AGE WHEN BOTTLED

BOTTLED ABV %

DATE OF DISTILLATION

DATE OF BOTTLING

BOTTLE NUMBER CASK NUMBER

CASK TYPE CASK SIZE

COMMENTS

MALT

DISTILLERY

SPEYSIDE ☐ HIGHLAND NORTHERN ☐ HIGHLAND EASTERN ☐ HIGHLAND WESTERN ☐ HIGHLAND SOUTHERN ☐ LOWLAND ☐ ISLAY ☐ ISLANDS ☐ CAMPBELTOWN ☐ IRELAND ☐ OTHER ☐

APPEARANCE

FULL STRENGTH

NOSE

TASTE

FIRST REDUCTION

NOSE

TASTE

SUPPLIED BY

CONTACT NAME/NUMBER

DATE OF PURCHASE

PRICE PAID – BOTTLE CASK

AGE WHEN BOTTLED

BOTTLED ABV %

DATE OF DISTILLATION

DATE OF BOTTLING

BOTTLE NUMBER CASK NUMBER

CASK TYPE CASK SIZE

COMMENTS

MALT

DISTILLERY

SPEYSIDE ☐ HIGHLAND NORTHEEN ☐ HIGHLAND EASTERN ☐ HIGHLAND WESTERN ☐ HIGHLAND SOUTHERN ☐ LOWLAND ☐ ISLAY ☐ ISLANDS ☐ CAMPBELTOWN ☐ IRELAND ☐ OTHER ☐

APPEARANCE

FULL STRENGTH

NOSE

TASTE

FIRST REDUCTION

NOSE

TASTE

SUPPLIED BY

CONTACT NAME/NUMBER

DATE OF PURCHASE

PRICE PAID – BOTTLE   CASK

AGE WHEN BOTTLED

BOTTLED ABV %

DATE OF DISTILLATION

DATE OF BOTTLING

BOTTLE NUMBER   CASK NUMBER

CASK TYPE   CASK SIZE

COMMENTS

MALT

DISTILLERY

SPEYSIDE ☐ HIGHLAND NORTHERN ☐ HIGHLAND EASTERN ☐ HIGHLAND WESTERN ☐ HIGHLAND SOUTHERN ☐ LOWLAND ☐ ISLAY ☐ ISLANDS ☐ CAMPBELTOWN ☐ IRELAND ☐ OTHER ☐

APPEARANCE

FULL STRENGTH

NOSE

TASTE

FIRST REDUCTION

NOSE

TASTE

SUPPLIED BY

CONTACT NAME/NUMBER

DATE OF PURCHASE

PRICE PAID – BOTTLE CASK

AGE WHEN BOTTLED

BOTTLED ABV %

DATE OF DISTILLATION

DATE OF BOTTLING

BOTTLE NUMBER CASK NUMBER

CASK TYPE CASK SIZE

COMMENTS

MALT

DISTILLERY

SPEYSIDE ☐ HIGHLAND NORTHERN ☐ HIGHLAND EASTERN ☐ HIGHLAND WESTERN ☐ HIGHLAND SOUTHERN ☐ LOWLAND ☐ ISLAY ☐ ISLANDS ☐ CAMPBELTOWN ☐ IRELAND ☐ OTHER ☐

APPEARANCE

FULL STRENGTH

NOSE

TASTE

FIRST REDUCTION

NOSE

TASTE

SUPPLIED BY

CONTACT NAME/NUMBER

DATE OF PURCHASE

PRICE PAID – BOTTLE CASK

AGE WHEN BOTTLED

BOTTLED ABV %

DATE OF DISTILLATION

DATE OF BOTTLING

BOTTLE NUMBER CASK NUMBER

CASK TYPE CASK SIZE

COMMENTS

MALT

DISTILLERY

SPEYSIDE ☐ HIGHLAND NORTHERN ☐ HIGHLAND EASTERN ☐ HIGHLAND WESTERN ☐ HIGHLAND SOUTHERN ☐ LOWLAND ☐ ISLAY ☐ ISLANDS ☐ CAMPBELTOWN ☐ IRELAND ☐ OTHER ☐

APPEARANCE

FULL STRENGTH

NOSE

TASTE

FIRST REDUCTION

NOSE

TASTE

SUPPLIED BY

CONTACT NAME/NUMBER

DATE OF PURCHASE

PRICE PAID – BOTTLE CASK

AGE WHEN BOTTLED

BOTTLED ABV %

DATE OF DISTILLATION

DATE OF BOTTLING

BOTTLE NUMBER CASK NUMBER

CASK TYPE CASK SIZE

COMMENTS

MALT

DISTILLERY

SPEYSIDE ☐ HIGHLAND NORTHERN ☐ HIGHLAND EASTERN ☐ HIGHLAND WESTERN ☐ HIGHLAND SOUTHERN ☐ LOWLAND ☐ ISLAY ☐ ISLANDS ☐ CAMPBELTOWN ☐ IRELAND ☐ OTHER ☐

APPEARANCE

FULL STRENGTH

NOSE

TASTE

FIRST REDUCTION

NOSE

TASTE

SUPPLIED BY

CONTACT NAME/NUMBER

DATE OF PURCHASE

PRICE PAID – BOTTLE CASK

AGE WHEN BOTTLED

BOTTLED ABV %

DATE OF DISTILLATION

DATE OF BOTTLING

BOTTLE NUMBER CASK NUMBER

CASK TYPE CASK SIZE

COMMENTS

MALT

DISTILLERY

SPEYSIDE ☐ HIGHLAND NORTHERN ☐ HIGHLAND EASTERN ☐ HIGHLAND WESTERN ☐ HIGHLAND SOUTHERN ☐ LOWLAND ☐ ISLAY ☐ ISLANDS ☐ CAMPBELTOWN ☐ IRELAND ☐ OTHER ☐

APPEARANCE

FULL STRENGTH

NOSE

TASTE

FIRST REDUCTION

NOSE

TASTE

SUPPLIED BY

CONTACT NAME/NUMBER

DATE OF PURCHASE

PRICE PAID – BOTTLE CASK

AGE WHEN BOTTLED

BOTTLED ABV %

DATE OF DISTILLATION

DATE OF BOTTLING

BOTTLE NUMBER CASK NUMBER

CASK TYPE CASK SIZE

COMMENTS

MALT

DISTILLERY

SPEYSIDE ☐ HIGHLAND NORTHERN ☐ HIGHLAND EASTERN ☐ HIGHLAND WESTERN ☐ HIGHLAND SOUTHERN ☐ LOWLAND ☐ ISLAY ☐ ISLANDS ☐ CAMPBELTOWN ☐ IRELAND ☐ OTHER ☐

APPEARANCE

FULL STRENGTH

NOSE

TASTE

FIRST REDUCTION

NOSE

TASTE

SUPPLIED BY

CONTACT NAME/NUMBER

DATE OF PURCHASE

PRICE PAID – BOTTLE CASK

AGE WHEN BOTTLED

BOTTLED ABV %

DATE OF DISTILLATION

DATE OF BOTTLING

BOTTLE NUMBER CASK NUMBER

CASK TYPE CASK SIZE

COMMENTS

MALT

DISTILLERY

SPEYSIDE ☐ HIGHLAND NORTHERN ☐ HIGHLAND EASTERN ☐ HIGHLAND WESTERN ☐ HIGHLAND SOUTHERN ☐ LOWLAND ☐ ISLAY ☐ ISLANDS ☐ CAMPBELTOWN ☐ IRELAND ☐ OTHER ☐

APPEARANCE

FULL STRENGTH

NOSE

TASTE

FIRST REDUCTION

NOSE

TASTE

SUPPLIED BY

CONTACT NAME/NUMBER

DATE OF PURCHASE

PRICE PAID – BOTTLE CASK

AGE WHEN BOTTLED

BOTTLED ABV %

DATE OF DISTILLATION

DATE OF BOTTLING

BOTTLE NUMBER CASK NUMBER

CASK TYPE CASK SIZE

COMMENTS

MALT

DISTILLERY

SPEYSIDE ☐ HIGHLAND NORTHERN ☐ HIGHLAND EASTERN ☐ HIGHLAND WESTERN ☐ HIGHLAND SOUTHERN ☐ LOWLAND ☐ ISLAY ☐ ISLANDS ☐ CAMPBELTOWN ☐ IRELAND ☐ OTHER ☐

APPEARANCE

FULL STRENGTH

NOSE

TASTE

FIRST REDUCTION

NOSE

TASTE

SUPPLIED BY

CONTACT NAME/NUMBER

DATE OF PURCHASE

PRICE PAID – BOTTLE CASK

AGE WHEN BOTTLED

BOTTLED ABV %

DATE OF DISTILLATION

DATE OF BOTTLING

BOTTLE NUMBER CASK NUMBER

CASK TYPE CASK SIZE

COMMENTS

MALT

DISTILLERY

SPEYSIDE ☐ HIGHLAND NORTHERN ☐ HIGHLAND EASTERN ☐ HIGHLAND WESTERN ☐ HIGHLAND SOUTHERN ☐ LOWLAND ☐ ISLAY ☐ ISLANDS ☐ CAMPBELTOWN ☐ IRELAND ☐ OTHER ☐

APPEARANCE

FULL STRENGTH

NOSE

TASTE

FIRST REDUCTION

NOSE

TASTE

SUPPLIED BY

CONTACT NAME/NUMBER

DATE OF PURCHASE

PRICE PAID – BOTTLE CASK

AGE WHEN BOTTLED

BOTTLED ABV %

DATE OF DISTILLATION

DATE OF BOTTLING

BOTTLE NUMBER CASK NUMBER

CASK TYPE CASK SIZE

COMMENTS

MALT | DISTILLERY

SPEYSIDE ☐ HIGHLAND NORTHERN ☐ HIGHLAND EASTERN ☐ HIGHLAND WESTERN ☐ HIGHLAND SOUTHERN ☐ LOWLAND ☐ ISLAY ☐ ISLANDS ☐ CAMPBELTOWN ☐ IRELAND ☐ OTHER ☐

APPEARANCE

FULL STRENGTH

NOSE

TASTE

FIRST REDUCTION

NOSE

TASTE

SUPPLIED BY

CONTACT NAME/NUMBER

DATE OF PURCHASE

PRICE PAID – BOTTLE | CASK

AGE WHEN BOTTLED

BOTTLED ABV %

DATE OF DISTILLATION

DATE OF BOTTLING

BOTTLE NUMBER | CASK NUMBER

CASK TYPE | CASK SIZE

COMMENTS

MALT

DISTILLERY

SPEYSIDE ☐ HIGHLAND NORTHERN ☐ HIGHLAND EASTERN ☐ HIGHLAND WESTERN ☐ HIGHLAND SOUTHERN ☐ LOWLAND ☐ ISLAY ☐ ISLANDS ☐ CAMPBELTOWN ☐ IRELAND ☐ OTHER ☐

APPEARANCE

FULL STRENGTH

NOSE

TASTE

FIRST REDUCTION

NOSE

TASTE

SUPPLIED BY

CONTACT NAME/NUMBER

DATE OF PURCHASE

PRICE PAID – BOTTLE CASK

AGE WHEN BOTTLED

BOTTLED ABV %

DATE OF DISTILLATION

DATE OF BOTTLING

BOTTLE NUMBER CASK NUMBER

CASK TYPE CASK SIZE

COMMENTS

MALT

DISTILLERY

SPEYSIDE ☐ HIGHLAND NORTHERN ☐ HIGHLAND EASTERN ☐ HIGHLAND WESTERN ☐ HIGHLAND SOUTHERN ☐ LOWLAND ☐ ISLAY ☐ ISLANDS ☐ CAMPBELTOWN ☐ IRELAND ☐ OTHER ☐

APPEARANCE

FULL STRENGTH

NOSE

TASTE

FIRST REDUCTION

NOSE

TASTE

SUPPLIED BY

CONTACT NAME/NUMBER

DATE OF PURCHASE

PRICE PAID – BOTTLE CASK

AGE WHEN BOTTLED

BOTTLED ABV %

DATE OF DISTILLATION

DATE OF BOTTLING

BOTTLE NUMBER CASK NUMBER

CASK TYPE CASK SIZE

COMMENTS

MALT

DISTILLERY

SPEYSIDE ☐ HIGHLAND NORTHERN ☐ HIGHLAND EASTERN ☐ HIGHLAND WESTERN ☐ HIGHLAND SOUTHERN ☐ LOWLAND ☐ ISLAY ☐ ISLANDS ☐ CAMPBELTOWN ☐ IRELAND ☐ OTHER ☐

APPEARANCE

FULL STRENGTH

NOSE

TASTE

FIRST REDUCTION

NOSE

TASTE

SUPPLIED BY

CONTACT NAME/NUMBER

DATE OF PURCHASE

PRICE PAID – BOTTLE CASK

AGE WHEN BOTTLED

BOTTLED ABV %

DATE OF DISTILLATION

DATE OF BOTTLING

BOTTLE NUMBER CASK NUMBER

CASK TYPE CASK SIZE

COMMENTS

MALT

DISTILLERY

SPEYSIDE ☐ HIGHLAND NORTHERN ☐ HIGHLAND EASTERN ☐ HIGHLAND WESTERN ☐ HIGHLAND SOUTHERN ☐ LOWLAND ☐ ISLAY ☐ ISLANDS ☐ CAMPBELTOWN ☐ IRELAND ☐ OTHER ☐

APPEARANCE

FULL STRENGTH

NOSE

TASTE

FIRST REDUCTION

NOSE

TASTE

SUPPLIED BY

CONTACT NAME/NUMBER

DATE OF PURCHASE

PRICE PAID – BOTTLE CASK

AGE WHEN BOTTLED

BOTTLED ABV %

DATE OF DISTILLATION

DATE OF BOTTLING

BOTTLE NUMBER CASK NUMBER

CASK TYPE CASK SIZE

COMMENTS

MALT

DISTILLERY

SPEYSIDE ☐ HIGHLAND NORTHERN ☐ HIGHLAND EASTERN ☐ HIGHLAND WESTERN ☐ HIGHLAND SOUTHERN ☐ LOWLAND ☐ ISLAY ☐ ISLANDS ☐ CAMPBELTOWN ☐ IRELAND ☐ OTHER ☐

APPEARANCE

FULL STRENGTH

NOSE

TASTE

FIRST REDUCTION

NOSE

TASTE

SUPPLIED BY

CONTACT NAME/NUMBER

DATE OF PURCHASE

PRICE PAID – BOTTLE CASK

AGE WHEN BOTTLED

BOTTLED ABV %

DATE OF DISTILLATION

DATE OF BOTTLING

BOTTLE NUMBER CASK NUMBER

CASK TYPE CASK SIZE

COMMENTS

MALT DISTILLERY

SPEYSIDE ☐ HIGHLAND NORTHERN ☐ HIGHLAND EASTERN ☐ HIGHLAND WESTERN ☐ HIGHLAND SOUTHERN ☐ LOWLAND ☐ ISLAY ☐ ISLANDS ☐ CAMPBELTOWN ☐ IRELAND ☐ OTHER ☐

APPEARANCE

FULL STRENGTH

NOSE

TASTE

FIRST REDUCTION

NOSE

TASTE

SUPPLIED BY

CONTACT NAME/NUMBER

DATE OF PURCHASE

PRICE PAID – BOTTLE CASK

AGE WHEN BOTTLED

BOTTLED ABV %

DATE OF DISTILLATION

DATE OF BOTTLING

BOTTLE NUMBER CASK NUMBER

CASK TYPE CASK SIZE

COMMENTS

MALT

DISTILLERY

SPEYSIDE ☐ HIGHLAND NORTHERN ☐ HIGHLAND EASTERN ☐ HIGHLAND WESTERN ☐ HIGHLAND SOUTHERN ☐ LOWLAND ☐ ISLAY ☐ ISLANDS ☐ CAMPBELTOWN ☐ IRELAND ☐ OTHER ☐

APPEARANCE

FULL STRENGTH

NOSE

TASTE

FIRST REDUCTION

NOSE

TASTE

SUPPLIED BY

CONTACT NAME/NUMBER

DATE OF PURCHASE

PRICE PAID – BOTTLE CASK

AGE WHEN BOTTLED

BOTTLED ABV %

DATE OF DISTILLATION

DATE OF BOTTLING

BOTTLE NUMBER CASK NUMBER

CASK TYPE CASK SIZE

COMMENTS

MALT

DISTILLERY

SPEYSIDE ☐ HIGHLAND NORTHERN ☐ HIGHLAND EASTERN ☐ HIGHLAND WESTERN ☐ HIGHLAND SOUTHERN ☐ LOWLAND ☐ ISLAY ☐ ISLANDS ☐ CAMPBELTOWN ☐ IRELAND ☐ OTHER ☐

APPEARANCE

FULL STRENGTH

NOSE

TASTE

FIRST REDUCTION

NOSE

TASTE

SUPPLIED BY

CONTACT NAME/NUMBER

DATE OF PURCHASE

PRICE PAID – BOTTLE CASK

AGE WHEN BOTTLED

BOTTLED ABV %

DATE OF DISTILLATION

DATE OF BOTTLING

BOTTLE NUMBER CASK NUMBER

CASK TYPE CASK SIZE

COMMENTS

MALT

DISTILLERY

SPEYSIDE ☐ HIGHLAND NORTHERN ☐ HIGHLAND EASTERN ☐ HIGHLAND WESTERN ☐ HIGHLAND SOUTHERN ☐ LOWLAND ☐ ISLAY ☐ ISLANDS ☐ CAMPBELTOWN ☐ IRELAND ☐ OTHER ☐

APPEARANCE

FULL STRENGTH

NOSE

TASTE

FIRST REDUCTION

NOSE

TASTE

SUPPLIED BY

CONTACT NAME/NUMBER

DATE OF PURCHASE

PRICE PAID – BOTTLE CASK

AGE WHEN BOTTLED

BOTTLED ABV %

DATE OF DISTILLATION

DATE OF BOTTLING

BOTTLE NUMBER CASK NUMBER

CASK TYPE CASK SIZE

COMMENTS

MALT

DISTILLERY

SPEYSIDE ☐ HIGHLAND NORTHERN ☐ HIGHLAND EASTERN ☐ HIGHLAND WESTERN ☐ HIGHLAND SOUTHERN ☐ LOWLAND ☐ ISLAY ☐ ISLANDS ☐ CAMPBELTOWN ☐ IRELAND ☐ OTHER ☐

APPEARANCE

FULL STRENGTH

NOSE

TASTE

FIRST REDUCTION

NOSE

TASTE

SUPPLIED BY

CONTACT NAME/NUMBER

DATE OF PURCHASE

PRICE PAID – BOTTLE CASK

AGE WHEN BOTTLED

BOTTLED ABV %

DATE OF DISTILLATION

DATE OF BOTTLING

BOTTLE NUMBER CASK NUMBER

CASK TYPE CASK SIZE

COMMENTS

MALT

DISTILLERY

SPEYSIDE ☐ HIGHLAND NORTHERN ☐ HIGHLAND EASTERN ☐ HIGHLAND WESTERN ☐ HIGHLAND SOUTHERN ☐ LOWLAND ☐ ISLAY ☐ ISLANDS ☐ CAMPBELTOWN ☐ IRELAND ☐ OTHER ☐

APPEARANCE

FULL STRENGTH

NOSE

TASTE

FIRST REDUCTION

NOSE

TASTE

SUPPLIED BY

CONTACT NAME/NUMBER

DATE OF PURCHASE

PRICE PAID – BOTTLE CASK

AGE WHEN BOTTLED

BOTTLED ABV %

DATE OF DISTILLATION

DATE OF BOTTLING

BOTTLE NUMBER CASK NUMBER

CASK TYPE CASK SIZE

COMMENTS

MALT

DISTILLERY

SPEYSIDE ☐ HIGHLAND NORTHEEN ☐ HIGHLAND EASTERN ☐ HIGHLAND WESTERN ☐ HIGHLAND SOUTHERN ☐ LOWLAND ☐ ISLAY ☐ ISLANDS ☐ CAMPBELTOWN ☐ IRELAND ☐ OTHER ☐

APPEARANCE

FULL STRENGTH

NOSE

TASTE

FIRST REDUCTION

NOSE

TASTE

SUPPLIED BY

CONTACT NAME/NUMBER

DATE OF PURCHASE

PRICE PAID – BOTTLE　　CASK

AGE WHEN BOTTLED

BOTTLED ABV %

DATE OF DISTILLATION

DATE OF BOTTLING

BOTTLE NUMBER　　CASK NUMBER

CASK TYPE　　CASK SIZE

COMMENTS

MALT

DISTILLERY

SPEYSIDE ☐ HIGHLAND NORTHERN ☐ HIGHLAND EASTERN ☐ HIGHLAND WESTERN ☐ HIGHLAND SOUTHERN ☐ LOWLAND ☐ ISLAY ☐ ISLANDS ☐ CAMPBELTOWN ☐ IRELAND ☐ OTHER ☐

APPEARANCE

FULL STRENGTH

NOSE

TASTE

FIRST REDUCTION

NOSE

TASTE

SUPPLIED BY

CONTACT NAME/NUMBER

DATE OF PURCHASE

PRICE PAID – BOTTLE CASK

AGE WHEN BOTTLED

BOTTLED ABV %

DATE OF DISTILLATION

DATE OF BOTTLING

BOTTLE NUMBER CASK NUMBER

CASK TYPE CASK SIZE

COMMENTS

INDEX OF PAGE ENTRIES

PAGE	MALT	PAGE	MALT
31		37	
32		38	
33		39	
34		40	
35		41	
36		42	

PAGE	MALT	PAGE	MALT
43		54	
44		55	
45		56	
46		57	
47		58	
48		59	
49		60	
50		61	
51		62	
52		63	
53		64	

PAGE	MALT	PAGE	MALT
65		76	
66		77	
67		78	
68		79	
69		80	
70		81	
71		82	
72		83	
73		84	
74		85	
75		86	

PAGE	MALT	PAGE	MALT
87		98	
88		99	
89		100	
90		101	
91		102	
92		103	
93		104	
94		105	
95		106	
96		107	
97		108	

PAGE	MALT
109	
110	
111	
112	
113	
114	
115	
116	
117	
118	
119	

PAGE	MALT
120	
121	
122	
123	
124	
125	
126	
127	
128	
129	
130	

PAGE	MALT	PAGE	MALT
131		138	
132		139	
133		140	
134		141	
135		142	
136		143	
137		144	